PAUL ELLIS

LETTERS FROM
JESUS

Finding Good News
in Christ's Letters to the Churches

KINGSPRESS
Beach Haven, New Zealand

Letters from Jesus: Finding Good News in Christ's Letters to the Churches

ISBN: 978–1–927230–47–3
Copyright © 2019 by Paul Ellis

Published by KingsPress, Beach Haven, New Zealand. This title is also available in ebook form. Visit www.KingsPress.org for information.

Cover layout and design by Jelena Mirkovic Jankovic.

Version: 1.0 (April 2019)

Endorsements

I don't know anyone who hasn't approached the book of Revelation without fear and foreboding – and mostly avoided it even after reading it. My friend, Paul Ellis, has written a monumentally important book that will deliver the reader from confusion and fear to eager fascination and joy – I've never read anything like it. I love the way Paul writes and communicates the truth with wit and humor, while his scholarly diligence undergirds and shines through everything he offers. I love this book!

- RALPH HARRIS
    Best-selling author of *Life According to Perfect* and *God's Astounding Opinion of You*

Paul Ellis is a provocative writer because he writes stubbornly about a provocative subject: grace. And the grace he writes about isn't the safe, tame version that many of us grew up hearing about. It's the real stuff – the no-strings-attached kind, the one without "buts and brakes." He understands that Christianity is not good advice for "good" people, but rather good news for bad people. He understands that there is nothing we can do or fail to do that will ever tempt God to leave us or forsake us. He understands that the God of grace has forgiven the sins of our yesterdays, today's, and tomorrows – that because of Jesus, God doesn't remember the sins we can't forget. He understands the seemingly too-good-to-be-true nature of grace that inseparably connects us to the God of repeat offenders. Thank you, Paul, for reminding me, in *Letters from Jesus*, that "it is finished." I keep forgetting.

- TULLIAN TCHIVIDJIAN
    Author of *One Way Love: Inexhaustible Grace for an Exhausted World*

Paul Ellis does an amazing job of revealing the heart of Jesus in these often very misunderstood letters. Legalists have used these passages of scripture to strike fear into the hearts of believers for many years. Paul helps us understand what Jesus is saying to his early church by taking the culture and context of each letter and breaking it down line by line. We get a clearer picture of what Jesus was saying and also how it applies to us today. I really enjoyed this book and it ministered to me greatly. I would encourage anyone who has wrestled with these scriptures to check out *Letters from Jesus*.

- JEREMIAH JOHNSON
    Author of *Freedom* and Senior Pastor at Grace Point Church, KY

Wow! Wow! I related to every letter to every church. At one time I could have earned the title, "Queen of the Laodicean Church." But once I made my trade for gold from Jesus, my eyes were opened to grace, and I became a hot mess of blubbering gratefulness. I soon found myself rich, but kicked to the curb because I couldn't preach the cheap law anymore. Abandoned, but not forsaken, Jesus has been reading those first six letters to me for years and encouraging me to keep on keepin' on. I just didn't realize they were already in the Bible! Paul, thanks for finding them in the attic and dusting them off for me! This book is deep encouragement for anyone who believes and preaches the gospel without compromise.

- TRICIA GUNN
  Author of *Unveiling Jesus* and Founder of Parresia

I used to read Jesus' letters to the churches and cringe. Somehow I knew there was something I was missing. Thank you, Paul! Finally a grace-centered explanation giving the reader both a historical, applicable, and relevant interpretation of these important but often misunderstood chapters. I highly recommend this groundbreaking work!

- NATE TANNER
  Evangelist and President at L3 International Ministries

Letters from Jesus, is one of the most insightful and refreshing books I have had the privilege of reading. Paul Ellis does a masterful job of revealing God's heart and purpose regarding the true meaning of these seven letters. These letters were not only meant for the early church but help open our eyes so we can also escape the same religious traps they succumbed to. I highly recommend Paul's new book *Letters from Jesus*, and I believe it will become a classic. It is a book I plan on reading over and over again. It is packed with wisdom, revelation, and truth that we all need today.

- ED ELLIOTT
  President of Word of Life World Outreach aka "The Vagabond Evangelist"

Contents

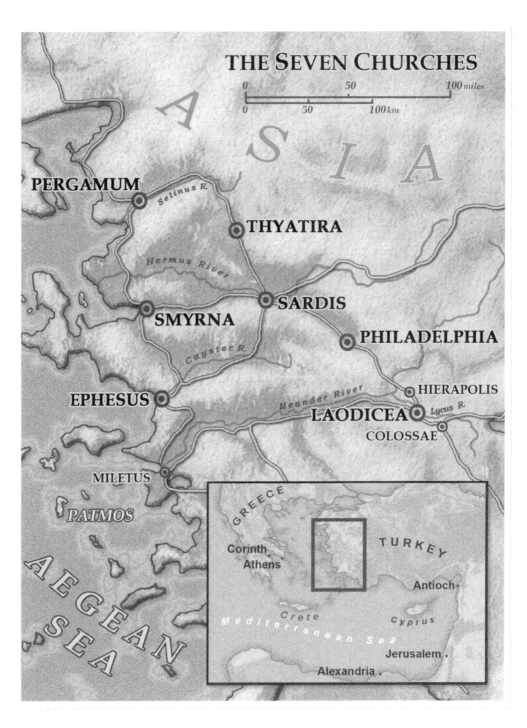

The seven churches of Asia

The Lost Letters of Jesus

In the creviced hills east of the Sea of Galilee, a kibbutznik stumbled on the neck of a partially buried earthen jar. Inside the jar was a roll of parchment. Experts at the Hebrew University of Jerusalem examined the parchment and found letters written by someone claiming to be the Son of God. The letters were dated to the first century, and all the evidence indicated that they had been written by Jesus Christ.

A media frenzy followed. Within days the letters were translated into every language known to man. They were circulated online and everybody read them. The letters, revealing a side of Christ that few had seen, triggered a theological cataclysm. Seminarians squabbled, boards bickered, and churches split. Yet many believed that God was sending humanity a much-needed message of love and hope. Feuds ended and wars ceased. So many people turned to Christ on account of these letters that media outlets labeled their discovery the most important event in Christendom since the resurrection.

Everything above is a fiction. I wrote it as a thought experiment, a kind of what-if question. What if someone did discover letters from Jesus? Would you be excited? Would you read them? Of course you would. They're *letters from Jesus*. How often do you get mail from the Son of God?

How might the world react to such a discovery? I ask because we do, in fact, have seven lost letters from Jesus. They've been hidden in plain sight for 2,000 years. I am referring to Christ's letters to the seven churches, which are recorded in the Book of Revelation. I call them lost because many people don't know that Jesus sent seven letters, and those who do tend to leave them buried and unread in the back of their Bibles.

It is a miracle these letters from Jesus have survived. They have outlasted the language in which they were written and the cities to which they were sent. In the intervening centuries, empires have risen and fallen; civilizations have come and gone. The letters from Jesus have come to us via a long chain of scribes, copyists, archivists, translators, editors, and publishers. We are blessed to have these letters, but some of their meaning has been lost in translation. How do I know? Because those who love Christ fear his letters. They see Jesus with burning eyes and sharp swords and they don't recognize him. The Jesus in the Gospels drew people with grace, but the Jesus in these letters seems like Rambo on a rampage. Something doesn't add up.

What happened to Jesus?

Many people dismiss the seven Revelation letters as too hard, too strange, or too scary. From time to time they may hear a sermon or a teaching on one of the letters, and while the message may give them a measure of joy, it also leaves them confused and anxious. "Did Jesus really say that?"

Take the letter to the Laodiceans. In it Jesus says the Laodiceans are lukewarm and poor, and he is about to vomit them up. What does Jesus have against poor people, you wonder. And how do I avoid being spewed out?

In the letter to Sardis, Jesus describes himself as a thief. Jesus is a thief?!

In the letter to Pergamum, he says he's coming to wage war with a sword. With a what now?!

In the letter to Thyatira, Jesus says he will cast a certain lady onto a bed of suffering and slay her children with death. Has Jesus gone rogue? Has he joined the Dark Side?

In our confusion we turn to religion for answers and learn that sometimes the Lord directs his anger against his church. "If he punishes us, it's for our own good." So he loves us, but he also beats us. Hallelujah.

We are told that the letters contain a mix of praises and rebukes. "Do good, and God will reward you. But do bad, and the Lord will punish you." In other words, God drives us like donkeys using sticks and carrots. Hee-haw.

And how are we to respond to these letters? Religion offers an unequivocal answer: Work harder for the Lord. "The Ephesians slacked off, while the Laodiceans cooled off. You'd best lift your game or you will be cast off."

I don't know about you, but none of this sounds like good news to me. In fact, it sounds exactly like the sort of message that leaves people burdened with debilitating guilt and shame.

I have a different take on the letters from Jesus. Contrary to what you may have heard, I believe they are good news from start to finish. They are seven unqualified revelations of the extreme goodness and radical favor of God. Manmade religion hurts people, but the gospel of Jesus found in these letters has the power to save, heal, and deliver. And I'm not just saying that because I want you to read my book. I know for a fact that these letters from Jesus can change your life. They certainly changed mine.

How did I get here?

About ten years ago I was wrestling with Christ's letter to the Laodiceans. I couldn't make sense of it. Sure, I knew what it was supposed to mean. I had preached the "Get on fire for God" message many times. Problem was, it no longer felt true. It didn't resonate with my growing understanding of God's grace. Like many Christians, I was tempted to put the letter in the too hard basket. I just couldn't make sense of what Jesus was saying to those poor Laodiceans.

So I prayed. I asked the Holy Spirit for help. "What is Jesus saying in this letter? Who is in danger of being spewed out? And how do I reconcile what Jesus said (in his letter) with what Jesus did (on the cross)?" The next moment it was like scales fell from my eyes. The Spirit of Grace opened the eyes of my understanding and I saw treasures in the letter I had never seen before. And these weren't obscure little gems that required knowledge of archaic Greek or ancient customs. They were great big, obvious, gospel truths. How had I missed them?

I shared my new understanding with a group of pastor friends and they responded with excitement and joy. They encouraged me to take things further, so I shared what the Spirit had shown me in a brand new blog called Escape to Reality.

That Laodicean article launched a platform for the gospel that has been visited millions of times by people in every country in the world. Countless people have written to tell me they've been set free by the good news of God's unconditional love and grace. To this day, I regularly hear from readers who say, "My life was changed by what you wrote about the lukewarm Laodiceans." I give God all the credit. Jesus wrote the letter to the Laodiceans, not me. All I did was read it with the Spirit's aid. I asked; he helped.

Reading that letter from Jesus was a milestone in my journey towards grace. After that, everything changed. It was like the Holy Spirit gave me new eyes. From then on, every verse in the Bible looked different and better. I changed careers and became a writer. I kind of had to. This good news that I was seeing on every page was too good not to share. And the writing came easy. All I had to do was remove the manmade additives that ruin the gospel and let the undiluted words of scripture do what they were always intended to do, which is point to Jesus.

So far I have written articles covering more than a thousand scriptures. (They're on the blog.) But it all started with Laodicea. After I asked the Lord about Laodicea, I asked about Ephesus and the other churches as well. Because of what he showed me, I'm no longer troubled by these letters. You shouldn't be either. I now realize the letters to the churches are timeless love letters from Jesus to us. They are replete with unfathomable grace, and they speak to the deepest needs of our hearts.

And the strange thing is hardly anyone seems to know this.

The Jesus of the Gospels

The seven letters of Jesus comprise two of the most studied chapters in the Bible. Countless sermons have been preached about them. Numerous books have been written. While writing this one, I read several dozen commentaries. I am grateful for the archeologists, linguists, and historians who help us understand the first-century context in which the letters were written. But in many of the books I read and sermons I heard, I encountered a mixed-up Jesus who accepts us one day, but rejects us the next. He invites us to rest, but he wants us to work. He heals us, but he slays us. He forgives our sins, but he holds them against us. He paid it all, but he expects us to pay him back. He loves us, but he doesn't.

It's confusing and unsettling because it's untrue. It's discordant because it is out of tune with the Spirit of Grace. The Jesus of the Gospels invited all to freely enter his kingdom, but the Jesus I heard about was selling tickets. "To make the cut, you have to pass the overcoming test, the no-compromise test, and the loyalty test. You have to get on fire, display some passion, and never, ever quit. If you're not faithful unto death, don't expect a crown of life. Martyrdom and suffering are the cost of entry."

Could it be that the Jesus of the seven letters is a different Jesus? Or have we been reading these letters wrong?

I wrote this book so that you might see that the Jesus of the Gospels *is* the Jesus of the seven letters. There is no difference. Jesus does not change from one day to the next, and he certainly did not change between the first and last books of the New Testament. As in the Gospels, the Jesus of the seven letters is a deliverer, champion, redeemer, and savior.

So it's the same Jesus, but it's also a different Jesus. The Jesus in the Gospels was born in a stable and died on a cross, but the Jesus in these letters is clothed in glory and sitting at the right hand of the Almighty. In the Gospels, Jesus referred to himself as the Son of Man, but in these letters he is the Son of God (see Rev. 2:18). Gospel Jesus is meek and mild, but this one is the Lord above all.

The Jesus of the seven letters is not the Jesus you heard about in Sunday School, the one who got pushed around by religious bullies and was broken and killed for our iniquities. No sir. This is the Risen Lord with eyes aflame, feet like bronze, and words that fall like hammers.

The Jesus of the Seven Letters

You may know the Jesus of the Gospels, but how well do you know the Jesus of the seven letters?

Did you know the New Testament records 2,000 words that were spoken by Jesus after he ascended to heaven? And did you know that most of these words are found in the seven letters? If you're one of the many people who hasn't read these letters, you're missing out on most of what Jesus has said since returning to heaven.

"But these letters were not meant for me." That's not true. The letters from Jesus were sent to the seven churches, but they contain messages for all of us, as we shall see. At the end of each letter, we will ask a couple of questions: What was Jesus saying to them, and what is Jesus saying to us?

In these letters, the Son of God dispenses life-giving words to: the weary and worn out (Ephesus), those living in the shadow of death (Smyrna), victims of bullying and those facing questions of conscience (Pergamum), the misguided who mishandle grace (Thyatira), those worried about their eternal security (Sardis), the powerless who think they have nothing to offer (Philadelphia), and those who are confused over the balance between law and grace (Laodicea). The letters are short but deep. As we unpack them in this book, we will find answers to many common questions: What does God expect from me? Does he care that I'm bone tired? Is he angry at my fears and failings? How do I know what the

Spirit is saying? How do I overcome life's trials? How can I face death without fear? What makes me worthy to walk with the Lord? Am I lukewarm? Does God punish me when I sin? If I stumble, will Jesus erase my name from his book? What if I deny him in a moment of weakness?

Tough questions, but the Jesus of the seven letters has good answers.

The letters of Jesus were never lost, but maybe their meaning has been lost on you. My hope is that as you read this book, the Spirit of Christ will give you understanding so that you may know him better. My prayer is that you will see Jesus in his letters.

But before we start, there is one important question we must ask: How do we read the letters from Jesus?

How to Read the Seven Letters

The actor Charlie Chaplin once entered a Charlie Chaplin lookalike contest and lost.[1] Why did Charlie Chaplin go unrecognized? Surely it was because we see what we expect to see. No one expected the real Charlie Chaplin to show up, so no one saw him when he did. Even so, it was quite an oversight. It's not like Charlie Chaplin was unknown. At the time, he was the most recognizable person on earth. Along with the other contestants, he would have been scrutinized to see how much like Chaplin he was. Yet nobody saw him.

The same principle applies when we come to the scriptures: We see what we expect to see. Or to put it another way, what you believe determines what you see. If you believe the Bible is full of rules we must keep to please the Lord, you will find rules whenever you read the Bible. And if you believe we must work hard or avoid sin to please God, you will find tasks to complete and sins to avoid on every page. Our beliefs filter what we see.

Me? I expect to see Jesus on every page and in every book from Genesis to Revelation. Is this not why the Bible was written—to reveal Jesus? Is it not his story? All the histories, poems, laws, songs, and stories of the Old and New Testaments point to him. To paraphrase Augustine, "Jesus is in the old concealed; Jesus is in the new revealed." Or to quote *The Jesus Storybook Bible*, every story whispers his name.

How to read scripture in context

Any preacher worth their salt will tell you that we need to read the Bible in context, but what is the proper context? Jesus is. He is the Living Word who gives meaning to the written word. The word context means weave together. We take the words and weave a story. Try and weave a story from scripture without the central thread of Jesus Christ and you could end up with a bad story. This is why we need to wear *Son*-glasses when reading scripture. We don't read the Bible to find principles for success (although it has plenty) or rules for living (ditto); we read it to connect with the Author of Life. We read it to grow in the grace and knowledge of Jesus Christ.

This seems obvious, no? But it is not common practice, particularly when it comes to reading the letters from Jesus.

Some interpret Christ's letters through historical, cultural, or linguistic lenses. Others prefer a prophetic or dispensational approach. A lens, or hermeneutic, to use the proper word, is a tool for constructing a story. If your lens helps you to grow in the grace and knowledge of Jesus, it's a good lens. But if your lens distracts you from Jesus, it's a dud. On the road to Emmaus, Jesus interpreted "all the scriptures," from Moses to the prophets, through a Christocentric hermeneutic (Luke 24:27). He said, "This is all about me." If the entire Old Testament, from Moses to the prophets, is all about Jesus, then so is the New Testament, from Matthew to Revelation.

With that in mind, let's consider the first four words of the Book of Revelation:

The Revelation of Jesus Christ... (Revelation 1:1a)

What is the Book of Revelation about? It's about Jesus. It is the revelation of Jesus Christ. Sure, it's about other things as well. But like the rest of scripture, it is principally about Jesus, who has come and is coming again.

The New Testament was written by people who saw Jesus, and this is true of John's Revelation. "I saw one like a son of man," said John, "and his face shone like the sun," (Rev. 1:13, 16). The old apostle saw Jesus in all his glory and was told to "write what you see" (Rev. 1:11). When we read Revelation, we are reading *what John saw*. If we see what John saw – Jesus – we are reading correctly. If we see something else, such as a projection of ourselves and our shortcomings, we are reading it wrong.

It is tempting for us to study the scriptures to find *stuff we must do*, but a healthier approach is to see what Jesus has done and is now doing. For instance, in one of the seven letters, we find Jesus walking among the lampstands. It sounds mysterious, but it's a powerful revelation of Christ-with-us. The lampstands, Jesus explains, are the churches. Jesus is walking among the churches.

How does this help us?

It sets us free from the false image of an aloof and distant Lord. Jesus is among the lampstands meaning he is with us and for us. It's good news for those who feel far from God.

14

We are changed by beholding Jesus, so in this book we are going to behold Jesus. We are going to see aspects of Jesus that are found nowhere else in scripture. And we're going to hear him say things that are not recorded any other place. Best of all, we are going to encounter his heart. While the Gospels record the words and actions of Jesus, his letters reveal his thoughts and they are good.

Context is also defined by the audience, and here we must ask, who wrote the seven letters, when did he write them, to whom were they written, and why?

Who wrote the seven letters?

The letters are from Jesus, but they were recorded by John. Jesus spoke the words and John wrote them down. (Or did he? We'll examine this question in Appendix 1.)

You may recall that John was a superstar. He walked with Christ. He stood on the Mount of Transfiguration, and he saw the empty tomb. But that was a lifetime ago. Since those glory days, John had seen all his fellow apostles murdered, and he himself had been banished to a rocky island. John's best years were behind him. The man who had been at the center was now at the edge. Old and all but forgotten, John had nothing to look forward to but a lonely death. Then one day Jesus gave John a heavenly vision of such splendor that we're still talking about it 2,000 years later.

John recording the letters

John was on the island of Patmos when he saw his vision (Rev. 1:9), and he wrote it down towards the end of the first century, probably around the years of AD95/96. This date is not universally accepted, but it is supported by the majority of church fathers and historians. (See Appendix 1: When Were the Seven Letters Written?) What was the significance of this date? At the turn of the first century, the early church was in danger of being snuffed out. The "mother church" in Jerusalem had gone; all but one of the original apostles had died; and John was stuck on a barren rock in the middle of the sea. Would the young church survive? Of course it did survive, and one of the reasons it did was because Jesus sent letters from heaven. In a time without Bibles, these letters were tremendously important. You can be sure the early church placed far more importance on them than we do. Which is surprising, because we might not be here if they hadn't.

To whom were the letters written?

Jesus instructed John to record the vision in a book and then send that book along with some letters to "the seven churches that are in Asia" (Rev. 1:4). This is not the Asia we know, but the Roman Province of Asia that was situated on the western end of the Anatolian peninsula in modern Turkey. The letters were for the churches in Ephesus, Smyrna, Pergamum, Thyatira, Sardis, Philadelphia, and Laodicea (Rev. 1:11). What did these churches have in common? John probably knew them all. Having lived in Ephesus and traveled around the region, he would have been well acquainted with the challenges facing each one.

Look at the map of the seven cities found at the front of this book and you will see that the order of the letters begins with Ephesus, the city closest to John's exile on Patmos. The sequence then describes an n-shaped route that follows the coast up to Smyrna and Pergamum before heading inland to Thyatira and down to Sardis, Philadelphia, and Laodicea. This is the route that would've been taken by whoever delivered the letters. And who was that? It wasn't a postman, for no postal service existed in first-century Rome. (An imperial post service was used for government business.) The letters of the New Testament were carried by volunteers. According to the Scottish archeologist William Ramsay, Christian couriers were organized and hosted by the bishops or pastors for sending and receiving letters.[2]

John wrote a book and attached some letters from Jesus, and the whole package was sent from Patmos to Ephesus and from thence to the other six cities. Alternatively, John brought the package back to the mainland when he returned from exile. After settling back in his home church in Ephesus, he arranged for the delivery of the package to the other six cities.

Seven letters for seven churches, but this does not mean each church received only one letter. The seven letters were general letters circulated among all the churches. Thus the Laodiceans heard what Jesus said to the Ephesians and vice versa. There were no secrets here.

At the end of each letter, Jesus says, "Hear what the Spirit says to the churches." These letters were intended for *the* Church, meaning the whole body of Christ. They were written for you and me and your pastor and the organ lady and everyone who needs to know the love of the Lord. It's a mistake to think that the Laodiceans were the only lukewarm people in history or that wandering from your first love was a uniquely Ephesian problem. We all need to hear what the Spirit is saying through these letters from Jesus.

Why were the letters written?

The immediate reason was the church in Asia was going through tough times. Bad teaching was circulating inside the church and people were being led into harm's way. At the same time, the church was being attacked from no less than three external sources: religious Jews, idolatrous pagans, and imperious Romans. The Jews hated the church because it was full of uncircumcised law-breakers who revered a dead Nazarene as the living Son of God. Pagans opposed the church because it took customers away from the lucrative idol trade. And the Romans oppressed the church because they perceived it was a threat to the empire.[3]

Following Jesus in first-century Asia was no walk in the park. You risked losing your job, your home, even your life. Christians were beaten and murdered simply for believing in the name of the Lord. It must have broken Jesus' heart to see his church suffer, so he did something he'd never done: He sent seven letters. He responded to the bad news of their circumstances, by proclaiming the good news of his kingdom, and he did so using language and idioms that resonated with his readers.

Each letter opens with a picture of Jesus and closes with a promise. A picture and a promise: two things we need to navigate life's trials. When you're going through hard times, you need to see Jesus, who is above your circumstances, and when you're battling fear and anxiety, you need a promise you can cling to. The pictures and promises of Jesus stir our faith. They lift us from the depths of despair to the highlands of hope. They remind us that what we see is not all there is, and that no matter how bad things get, Jesus is always with us.

Yet the promises in these letters do even more than that. Collectively, they trace the full arc of humanity's story — a story that begins in the Paradise of Eden

(Ephesus) where we fell and reaped the curse of death (Smyrna). The story wanders through the manna-laden wilderness (Pergamum), to the heralded arrival of King with authority over the nations (Thyatira). The story then proceeds to the Day of Judgment and the opening of the Book of Life (Sardis), before leading us to a heavenly city, a heavenly temple (Philadelphia), and the very throne of God (Laodicea).[4]

The letters from Jesus speak to us at multiple levels. They address personal issues and universal ones. They unveil God's unchanging purposes for humanity, and they reveal your place in his eternal dream.

The seven letters from Jesus are no mere letters. They are the Gospel of Jesus as preached by Jesus. They are an invitation to partake in his divine life. And they reveal that no matter how history may twist and turn, God's good purposes will always come to pass.

Welcome to the letters from Jesus.

1. EPHESUS

To the angel of the church in Ephesus write: The One who holds the seven stars in his right hand, the One who walks among the seven golden lampstands, says this: "I know your deeds and your toil and perseverance, and that you cannot tolerate evil men, and you put to the test those who call themselves apostles, and they are not, and you found them to be false; and you have perseverance and have endured for my name's sake, and have not grown weary. But I have this against you, that you have left your first love. Therefore remember from where you have fallen, and repent and do the deeds you did at first; or else I am coming to you and will remove your lampstand out of its place – unless you repent. Yet this you do have, that you hate the deeds of the Nicolaitans, which I also hate. He who has an ear, let him hear what the Spirit says to the churches. To him who overcomes, I will grant to eat of the tree of life which is in the Paradise of God." (Revelation 2:1-7)

Take a trip to the Roman province of Asia and mighty Ephesus would be your first port of call. Situated on the mouth of the Cayster River on the Aegean Sea in the region of Ionia, the great trading city was the gateway to the East. It was a crossroads for trade and travelers and pilgrims visiting the famed Temple of Artemis or Artemision.

In the first century, Ephesus was the biggest and busiest seaport in Asia, and it was into this port that the Apostle Paul arrived on his first visit to the city (Acts 18:19). On that occasion he did not stay long, but on his second visit he stayed more than two years. In the hall of Tyrannus, the apostle held daily discussions, and the result was "all the Jews and Greeks in Asia heard the word of the Lord" (Acts 19:10). Indeed, Paul was so effective at leading people to Jesus that those in the Ephesian idol trade instigated a riot against him. As many as 24,000 angry Ephesians gathered in the theater to protest his ministry.[1]

As result of this unrest, Paul left Ephesus and went north to Macedonia. But the church he planted remained, and Paul briefly visited with the Ephesian elders on his final journey to Jerusalem (Acts 20:16-17).

Some years later, the Apostle John came to live in Ephesus, and it was to Ephesus that he returned after his exile on Patmos. According to the church historian Jerome of Stridon, John died at a ripe old age during the reign of the Emperor Trajan and was buried in Ephesus.[2] The church in Ephesus held a special place in the hearts of both apostles, and as we shall see, it was very dear to Jesus.

Revelation 2:1a To the angel of the church in Ephesus write:

Who is the angel of the church? Most likely the bishop (or lead elder or senior pastor if you prefer).

Each of the seven letters is addressed to an angel. An angel is literally a messenger, often divine, but not so here. (Why would Jesus send mail to heavenly beings? He's talking to people.) Recall that the letters were written by John and sent by him to the seven cities. John did not deliver the letters himself; he would've been far too old. He needed couriers, and they would need food and accommodation. If you've ever wondered why each of the seven letters is add-ressed to an angel, this is why. The angel, or bishop, was the person who received and fed the courier. He was the one who opened the letter from Jesus and read it out loud in church.

Who are the letters for? Since each letter is addressed to a single angel, some have con-cluded that the letters were meant exclusively for individual pastors. However, each letter ends with the phrase, "Hear what the Spirit says to the churches." Jesus is speaking to churches, not pastors. In fact, Jesus is speaking to *all* the churches (see Rev. 2:23), not just the seven churches of Asia. So these letters are for all believers.

Seven churches, seven angels

Then in his final letter Jesus says, "If *anyone* hears my voice and opens the door, I will come in" (Rev. 3:20). It's a universal invitation. The letters from Jesus are for all of us, good or bad, saved or unsaved, inside the church or out. No one is excluded.

Who was the angel of the church at Ephesus? Someone appointed by John.

The church in Ephesus had an impressive heritage. The first angel or leader was the Apostle Paul. He planted the church and led it for a while (Acts 20:31). After him, it was possibly led by Aquila and Priscilla (Acts 18:19, 1 Cor. 16:19), or Timothy (1 Tim. 1:3), then Tychicus (Eph. 6:21, 2 Tim. 4:12). According to the early church fathers, John himself may have led the church.[3] Since John was in Patmos when he wrote the letter, the current angel or bishop or pastor was probably someone appointed by John.

What is the meaning of the name Ephesus? Desirable, or desired one.[4] It's a fitting label for a letter full of desire. The Ephesians had left their first love. In this letter their First Love calls for the desired church to return to him.

Revelation 2:1b The One who holds the seven stars in his right hand, the One who walks among the seven golden lampstands, says this:

Who is the One holding the seven stars? Jesus. If the Bible is an art gallery, the Revelation letters are a special wing containing seven portraits of Jesus. These portraits are found at the beginning of each of the seven letters, and each is a treasure. For starters, they are self-portraits painted by Jesus himself. We are not hearing about Jesus second hand, and we are not seeing him through the eyes of another. This is Jesus revealing Jesus using word pictures found nowhere else. In the first portrait, we see Jesus is holding seven stars.

Who are the seven stars? The seven stars in the Lord's right hand are the angels or leaders of the seven churches (see Rev. 1:20). In scripture, those who teach the gospel of righteousness are called stars (Dan. 12:3), while false teachers are called wandering stars (Jude 1:13) — which kind of changes the meaning of the song, "I was born under a wandering star."

Why his right hand? The right hand of God signifies his power and strength. "Your right hand, O Lord, is majestic in power," sang Moses. "Your right hand, O Lord, shatters the enemy" (Ex. 15:6).

In the Psalms, God's right hand saves us (Ps. 60:5), holds us (Ps. 63:8), and shelters us (Ps. 17:7). His right hand is also the place of honor (Acts 2:33–34). So when Jesus tells the seven stars or bishops or pastors that he is holding them in his right hand, he is saying, "Fear not, for I am holding you with my mighty right hand."

This powerful image is reinforced in the letter to Sardis (Rev. 3:1), but in that letter a different word is used. In Sardis, Jesus is merely holding the seven stars, and no hand is mentioned. But in Ephesus, he is holding them *with strength* in his mighty right hand.[5] It's an image to reassure us. Jesus is saying, "I've got you, and no one can snatch you from my strong right hand" (see John 10:28).

What are the seven golden lampstands? The seven churches in Ephesus, Smyrna, Pergamum, Thyatira, Sardis, Philadelphia, and Laodicea (Rev. 1:20).

A lampstand, like a church, is a bearer of light. Like much else in Revelation — crowns, bowls, rods, censers, altars, streets and a city (Rev. 4:4, 5:8, 8:3, 21:15, 18, 21) — the lampstands are made of gold, meaning they are precious. In the Lord's eyes, any church, no matter how small or dysfunctional, is highly valued. If we were to view the church through the eyes of Jesus, we would see that it is much more than a collection of ragamuffins and misfits. The church is a treasure shining bright with the love of the Lord.

Where is Jesus walking? Among the lampstands or churches.

Before Jesus came, people pictured God walking in the heavens (Job 22:14). God was distant and "up there somewhere". But God's desire has always been to be with us. God walked with Adam and Eve in the cool of the evening (Gen. 3:8). He promised the Israelites, "I will walk among you and be your God" (Lev. 26:12). It rarely happened because every time he approached, we pushed him away. But Jesus is the fulfillment of God's eternal yearning. He is the man from heaven who walks with us by his Spirit here on earth. Jesus is not sitting on a cloud or wandering above the galaxies. He is among the lampstands, nurturing and enjoying his church.

What is the significance of this introduction? Although the Ephesian letter is famous for its rebuke—"you have left your first love"—Jesus wants us to know that he is not sitting in heaven firing thunderbolts of condemnation. He is with us, not against us; he is near us, not far away; and he holds us securely in his right hand.

What a wonderful preamble to a letter that might otherwise fill us with fear. Jesus is no distant deity dispensing divine dictates from on high. He is our nearest and dearest friend. He is our true love who is always with us and among us, and he will never let us go.

Revelation 2:2a I know your deeds and your toil and perseverance...

Why does Jesus say "I know"? Because he wants us to know that he cares for us and is intimately acquainted with the details of our lives.

"God is watching you. He knows what you did." This line evokes fear among some, but God's *knowing* reflects his *loving*. Because he loves you, your heavenly Father takes an interest in your life. The One who numbers the hairs on your head knows what you are going through. He knows the hardships and trials you are facing.

What deeds does Jesus know? *See commentary under Revelation 2:19a, on page 77.*

Why mention their deeds? He's encouraging them.

When you're working for the Lord, it's easy to feel underappreciated and unnoticed. Sometimes it can feel like nobody cares. But Jesus cares. He says, "I know how hard you are working. I see your deeds and toil."

Why mention their toil? Because they were working too hard.

Commentators make much of Jesus knowing the Ephesians' deeds and toil, as though an impressed Lord was recording their labors in his scorebook. But the original word for know simply means "I see".[6] It's not necessarily a commendation. In these letters, Jesus says, "I know" in regard to both good deeds (Rev. 2:19) and bad deeds (Rev. 3:1, 15).

So what is Jesus saying about the deeds of the Ephesians? Many believe that he is commending them for their hard work, but toil means labors, extreme weariness, and beating.[7] The Ephesians were taking a beating. They were working themselves to exhaustion. Why would the Lord commend them for that?

Jesus said, "Come to me, all who are weary and heavy-laden, and I will give you rest" (Matt. 11:28). The Ephesians were weary and heavy-laden. They were a busy church in a busy city. They were running all sorts of programs, ministries, and activities. They met every day of the week and twice on Sunday, and they were worn out.

Why mention their perseverance? Jesus commended the Philadelphians for keeping the word of *his* perseverance (Rev. 3:10), but the Ephesians were known for *their* perseverance. The former were impressed with the Lord's labor, while the latter were trying to impress him with their own. There is nothing wrong with perseverance if we're talking about the perseverance that comes from Jesus and bears good fruit (Rev. 1:9, Luke 8:15). But the toilsome perseverance of the Ephesians was not this sort of perseverance. Their endurance was based on their own resources, and the result was weariness and exhaustion.

Contrary to popular opinion, Jesus doesn't commend the Ephesians for working themselves into a miserable state. He does not say, "Well done you good and hard-working servants." But nor does he rebuke them for working too hard. He simply says, "I'm aware of how hard you are working." He's building up to something, as we will see in verse five.

> **Revelation 2:2b and that you cannot tolerate evil men, and you put to the test those who call themselves apostles, and they are not, and you found them to be false;**

Cannot tolerate? Tolerate is too mild a word. Other translations say the Ephesians could not bear evil men. They did not support them in any form, but they tested and exposed them as liars and frauds.

In these letters we are going to encounter a number of evil men and at least one evil woman. We will learn about the terrible damage they inflicted on the churches, especially in Pergamum and Thyatira. But one place where they were able to do no lasting harm was Ephesus.

What evil men? False apostles and Nicolaitans (see Rev. 2:6). The Apostle Paul warned the Ephesians to be on their guard against savage wolves who would come among them and try to harm the flock (Acts 20:28–31). Later, the Apostle John exhorted them to test the spirits so that they might discern the spirit of truth and the spirit of error (1 John 4:1–6). Did the Ephesians listen? They did! Among the travelers who passed through Ephesus, many claimed to be apostles or teachers, but the Ephesians tested them all. Any charlatan who darkened their doors was soon sent packing.

How did they test those claiming to be apostles? They might have asked questions like, "Do you believe we must live under law?" A Judaizer would have said yes. "Do you believe Jesus, God's Son, has come in the flesh?" A Gnostic would have said no. "Is it okay for Christians to participate in temple sacrifices?" A Nicolaitan would have said sure.

There were different kinds of false apostles but one thing they all had in common was greed (2 Pet. 2:14). They were in it for the money and they treated people as merchandise (see 2 Pet. 2:3, KJV). They ministered and carried on and did what they did to make themselves rich.

In what sense were these evil men false? They taught lies. Instead of preaching the truth that sets men free, the false apostles preached a perverted gospel that keeps men bound. They exploited people with made-up stories and introduced destructive doctrines (see 2 Pet. 2:1–3). Good teachers teach truth which leads to godliness (Tit. 1:1); bad ones teach falsehoods that stir up sin and death.

> **Revelation 2:3 and you have perseverance and have endured for my name's sake, and have not grown weary.**

What had they endured? Attacks from wolves in sheep's clothing.

In contrast with some of the other churches in Asia, there is no record of the Ephesians suffering persecution from hostile outsiders. But they did have to deal with divisive people inside the church, and that was no small thing. "From your own number, men will arise and distort the truth in order to draw away disciples after them," said Paul to the Ephesian elders, and the prospect of this happening brought tears to his eyes (Acts 20:30–31).

Bad teachers sink churches. Even when they are tested and dismissed, those who are left to pick up the pieces can become weary and jaded. Not the Ephesians. Although they had gone through testing times, they had endured. They did not become cynical and anti-church, and for this Jesus commends them.

For my name's sake? They did everything as unto the Lord and to make his name known. The Ephesians weren't empire-builders or guardians of correct doctrine. They were genuine believers with pure motives who wanted to lift up the name of Jesus in their city.

Were they weary or weren't they? In verse 2 Jesus says he knows their wearisome toil (if we read his words literally), but in verse 3 he says the Ephesians have not grown weary. It's confusing. Are the Ephesians weary or aren't they? A better way to read it is, "You have not wearied of your toil." Put it together with verse 2 and Jesus is saying, "You have been working so hard, yet you haven't quit. You're like the Energizer bunny who just keeps going."[8]

Were the Ephesians a model church? You might think so, but no. On the surface, the Ephesians appeared to be a successful church. They had a solid foundation laid by the Apostle of Grace, and they had been taught by the Apostle of Love. They worked hard, and they endured tough times. Best of all, their motives were pure. Everything they did was done in the name of the Lord. They seem like a model church, a paragon of Christian virtue. Yet they had one flaw that threatened to undo it all, and it was this shortcoming for which they became famous.

Revelation 2:4 But I have this against you, that you have left your first love.

Does Jesus hold our sins against us? *See Revelation 2:14 on page 61.*

What does it mean to leave your first love? They were no longer abiding in the love of God.

Jesus told the Ephesians, "You have left your first love," or *protos agape* to use the original phrase. *Agape* is a special word that describes the unconditional and self-sacrificing love of your heavenly Father. It is not a human form of love. Only God is *agape* (1 John 4:16). *Protos* means foremost. In the love equation, God's love comes first. He is the source of all love.

Your first love is not your love for God; it is God's love for you.

God's love is like sunshine. To say the Ephesians had left their first love is to say they had come out of the sun and were wandering in the shade. Like the prodigal son, they had walked away from their Father's love.

So the honeymoon was over? No. The old chestnut that new believers enjoy a honeymoon period before getting busy with the hard work of serving God is foreign to the gospel. We're supposed to abide, linger, and stay settled in the *agape* love of God. The honeymoon is the marriage. It's how we're meant to live.

Some say the Ephesians weren't loving each other as much as they should, but *agape* love is not something to give; it's something to receive. "This is *agape* love, not that we loved God, but that he loved us" (1 John 4:10). When Jesus says the Ephesians have left their *agape*, he's saying they are no longer receiving or abiding in God's love for them.

Perhaps you have heard it said that the Ephesians needed to reignite their love by picking up the pace. But they were already working themselves to exhaustion. If you were to ask the Ephesians, "Do you love the Lord?" they would say, "Of course we do. Look at all we're doing for him. Look at our deeds and toil and our zero-tolerance policy for bad doctrine."

Yet Jesus said they had left their first love. In the same way a wife may leave her husband, they had left Jesus. No doubt this announcement would have come as a shock to the Ephesians, just as it would be a shock to us. "I haven't left you, Lord. Look at how much I'm doing for you." And Jesus replies, "You've left."

The remarkable thing is that if anyone should have known this, it was the Ephesians. Their foundations had been laid by Paul, who wrote the celebrated and oft-quoted love chapter of 1 Corinthians 13. This same apostle had sent them a letter full of reminders about the height, depth, and breadth of God's *agape* love for them.[9] They also counted John, the Love Apostle, as one of their members.

Perhaps more than any other church, the Ephesian church was built on the revelation of Christ's great love; yet they wandered. They forgot the most important thing of all, which is to remain in the love of God. If we are to draw any lessons from their experience, the obvious one is this: If it can happen to an Ephesian, it can happen to us.

How can we wander from the love of God? By working ourselves to distraction and by trying to earn what God freely provides.

That Jesus would speak of the Ephesians' labor and lost love speaks volumes. These guys had too much going on. Living in the busiest city in Asia, they were burning the candle at both ends and burning themselves out in the process. What they were doing (working hard) was getting in the way of what they weren't doing (receiving from Jesus), which is why Jesus tells them to stop what they're doing and return to what they did before.

Revelation 2:5a Therefore remember from where you have fallen, and repent and do the deeds you did at first;

In what sense had they fallen? In the same way the Galatians fell from grace back under law, the Ephesians fell from the high place of their Father's love to the pit of dead works. They had fallen from the high way of the spirit to the low habits of the flesh. They were trying instead of trusting, striving instead of resting, and they had worn themselves out.

Had they fallen out of the kingdom? No, nor were they in any danger of doing so. When we fall, we fall *in* the kingdom. Although some fear the Ephesians were in danger of losing their salvation, the Lord who holds them in his powerful right hand will never let them go.

How do we return to our first love? Remember! This one word from the Lord shows us the way back to our Father's love and grace. Why did the prodigal head home? He remembered the height from which he had fallen. How do we get off the hamster wheel of wearisome religion? By remembering the love of God that we experienced when we first met Jesus.

It is worth noting that *remember* is the first imperative verb in the seven letters. (An imperative verb is an action word that is conveyed as a command. In the letter to the Ephesians there are three imperatives and they are all found in verse five: remember, repent, and do.) If you were to read these letters from Jesus looking for things to do, the first thing you would find is his exhortation to remember. This is significant. Jesus does not say, I want you to do more of this and do less of that. He is not an old covenant preacher laying down rules for better living. He is a new covenant preacher calling us to *remember*, recollect, and recall the way things were.

What are we supposed to remember? How much Jesus loves us. We are not to remember our faults and failings; we are to remember the Lord and the matchless demonstration of his love for us. Remember. This is the remedy for weary Ephesians and overworked Christians. It's the way home for those who have gone astray. Remember. Before we *repent* and before we *do* we need to remember who Jesus is and what he has done for us.

How do we repent? By renewing our minds and turning to God.

The word repent comes freighted with baggage. For some, repentance means turning from sin with tears of remorse, but that is not what Jesus is asking for here. Jesus wants the Ephesians to reconsider or think differently.[10] They are so preoccupied with works and toil that they have become distracted from their Source. Like anxious Martha, they need to rethink their priorities. They need to put first things first and do the one thing that matters.

"Repent and do," says Jesus. True repentance is a change in thinking that leads to a change in behavior. Jesus tells the Ephesians what to think (remember your first love), and then he tells them what to do (what you did at first). Jesus has no interest in holding an altar call where we come weeping and promising to change; he just wants us to change. And what brings lasting change? It's beholding Jesus among the lampstands. It's seeing the Lord as our nearest and dearest friend.

What deeds did we do at first? You enjoyed Jesus. When you first entered the kingdom you may have done nothing at all except recline at his feet. "Do that,"

Box 1.1: Are you saying we should not work?

Understand that there are two kinds of work. There is the kind the Apostle Paul did when he said, "I worked harder than them all," and there's the Ephesian kind that wears you out and distracts you from the love of God. What's the difference? Paul's labor was a response to the love of God. "The love of Christ compels me" (2 Cor. 5:14). The Apostle Paul traveled the world like a man consumed. He had to tell people about God's love because he would burst if he didn't. "I am compelled to preach. Woe to me if I do not preach the gospel!" (1 Cor. 9:16).

In contrast, the Ephesians, like many tired Christians, did what they did because of pressure—"it's expected of me"—and tradition—"that's the way we've always done it." Perhaps they felt obliged to live up to their spectacular heritage. Perhaps they thought they had to work as hard as Paul. We don't know what got them out of bed in the morning, but it wasn't the energizing love of God.

As we will see when we get to Revelation 2:19, there are faith works and dead works, and both kinds were evident in the Ephesian church. In the beginning, the church was known for "extraordinary miracles" done through Paul (Acts 19:11). A generation later it had become known for the dead and toilsome works of forgotten men. Big difference.

says the Lord. "Stop trying to give to me and receive from me. Follow Mary who sat rather than Martha who stressed."

Sadly, this is not the recommendation you will hear from those who elevate works above grace. "Doing what you did at first means praying and studying the word and evangelizing with the enthusiasm you had when you first came to Jesus." In other words, the hard-working Ephesians need to work even harder and so do you. "Through hard work we prove our love and maintain our good standing with God." Beware this graceless message! The mindless pursuit of religious busyness—even good works done in the name of Jesus—will distract you from the love of God. You'll end up with toiling in the kitchen instead of reclining with Jesus in the lounge.

The manmade Religion of Self Improvement says God's blessings are in front of us and we must press on to catch up to them. We have to pray more, witness more, and do more, before we can be blessed. But the greatest psalm ever written says God's goodness and lovingkindness are following us (see Ps. 23:6). They're right behind us. We don't have to push on to be blessed; we have to sit down. "He makes me lie down in green pastures" (Ps. 23:2).

The Good Shepherd is not the one pushing you to perform; he's trying to get you to rest. What happens when we yield to his gentle hand and lie down at rest in his presence? His goodness and grace catch up with us and we are blessed.

Revelation 2:5b or else I am coming to you and will remove your lampstand out of its place — unless you repent.

What does it mean to remove a lampstand? Change is coming. If the Ephesians don't change, Jesus will change them. If they don't return to him, he will come to them and carry them to a new place.

Many interpret this passage as a vague but dire warning to the Ephesians. "God will remove the light of his word. Their lamp will be snuffed out." But Jesus does not say he will punish or extinguish them. He doesn't even say he will remove them, with all the negative connotations that implies.[11] A literal reading of his words indicates he will *move* them out of their place. Since they are in a bad place of loveless exhaustion, how is this not a good thing?

Picture a loving husband whose wife is buried with work. Miserable, exhausted, and close to burnout she tells herself, "I'm doing this for us," but there is no *us*, not when she's working 100 hours a week and sleeping at the office. Her husband misses her terribly and is concerned for her health. He reminds her of the simpler times they enjoyed at the beginning and hopes she will return to him. But if she doesn't, he plans to come to her workplace, sweep her off her feet, and take her away. He'll sell the house and move to another town if he has to. He'll gladly give up everything for her.

That is the essence of what Jesus is saying here. "I am coming to you." If they don't return to their first love, their first love will come to them. This is good news, not bad news. It's sweet relief for the weary who can't find their way home.

What will Jesus do if they don't repent? He will take them to a quiet place.

When the disciples got too busy with ministry, the Jesus of the Gospels would say, "Come with me by yourselves to a quiet place and get some rest" (Mark 6:31). He's saying the same thing to his disciples in Ephesus. "Come away with me." The invitation was there, but the Ephesians had to respond. If they did nothing, perhaps because they were too tired to move or too invested to change, then the Lord-among-the-lampstands would come and lead them himself.

To those who have known the crushing weight of unholy expectations, these words of Jesus are a breath of fresh air. The weary Ephesians probably wept with relief when they heard them.

Revelation 2:6 Yet this you do have, that you hate the deeds of the Nicolaitans, which I also hate.

Who were the Nicolaitans? *See Revelation 2:15 on page 62.*

Does Jesus hate people? He doesn't hate the Nicolaitans; he hates their deeds. Interestingly, this is the only time in scripture that Jesus says he hates something. What terrible thing did the Nicolaitans do to arouse the Lord's hatred? We will find out when we get to Revelation 2:15.

Revelation 2:7a He who has an ear, let him hear what the Spirit says to the churches.

What does it mean to have an ear to hear? Truth dawns by revelation.

"He who has an ear let him hear what the Spirit is saying" is one of Jesus' favorite expressions. It's the punch line to each of the seven Revelation letters as well as several of his parables. He's saying, "Don't just hear my words; receive the Spirit of revelation."

Did you know it's possible to hear the words of Jesus and *not* hear what the Holy Spirit is saying? Think of it as a choice between earthly and heavenly wisdom. The former originates in our minds, while the latter comes from the Spirit. An example may help: If you read the Bible and come away with a list of things you must do to earn God's favor, then you have received earthly wisdom based on human understanding. Since your understanding comes from within, the focus will be on yourself. But if you come away with a revelation of Jesus — who he is and what he has done — then you have received heavenly wisdom. You have heard what the Spirit is saying because the Spirit always points to him.

What stops us from hearing the Spirit? An unbelieving heart.

Imagine you were one of the Ephesians hearing this letter from Jesus as it was read out in the assembly. Would you receive it as Christ's words? Or would you dismiss it as something John wrote? "Who does John think he is telling us we've left our first love? We don't need to repent. Look at all we're doing for the Lord." Close your heart to the message, perhaps because of the messenger, and you won't hear from the Spirit. You'll reject the truth that could set you free.

Not to put too fine a point on it, but how are you receiving the words of *this* book? Do you receive them as Holy Spirit-inspired? Or do you dismiss them as something written by a confused author? Do the words on these pages stir up anger? "I've invested too much of my life into ministry to heed all this nonsense about rest and receiving." Or do they release grace and healing? "Now I know why my walk with God has been so lifeless. I've wandered from my first love. I need to drop everything and return."

For as long as the Holy Spirit speaks through imperfect people, we will be tempted to ignore what he is saying. If only there was a definitive way to tell whether the message we're hearing is from the Holy Spirit. There is!

How do we know we are hearing what the Spirit is saying? We grow in the grace and knowledge of Jesus.

The Holy Spirit will always seek to reveal Jesus (John 15:26). If the message you are hearing directs you to Jesus, you can be sure that you are hearing from the Spirit of Christ.[12]

When Jesus says, "He who has an ear, let him hear," he's saying if we really listen we will hear more than a letter written for dead Ephesians. He's saying we can hear what the Spirit wants to say to us today. This is worth bearing in mind as we read these letters from the Lord. If we come away feeling condemned or proud, we've missed him. But if we come away praising God and established in the grace of Jesus, then we have heard what the Spirit is saying.

A message for all churches? Jesus is the leader of the Church with a capital C. His words to the Ephesians, Smyrneans, Pergamenes, etc. are for all churches. It's a mistake to think that wandering from your first love was a uniquely Ephesian problem. Every worn-out believer needs to hear from the Lord among the lampstands. We all need to hear what the Spirit is saying through these letters.

Revelation 2:7b To him who overcomes...

Who overcomes? The one who believes in Jesus.

A promise connected with overcoming is given at the end of each of the seven letters. This promise leads us to wonder, how do I overcome? And what happens if I don't? Is Jesus saying I can lose my salvation if I fail the overcoming test?

Some define overcoming as a list of things you must do. You have to prevail in life's trials, disarm spiritual enemies, and conquer every sin. You have to resist temptation, walk in daily victory, and defeat the devil. Do these things to your dying breath and you will earn the right to eat from the Tree of Life, but drop the ball and you'll be toast. This sort of thinking leads to stressed-out, overworked Christianity such as the Ephesians practiced, and it is not good news.

The word overcomes is a verb that means to conquer, prevail, or get the victory.[13] Look up the word in the dictionary and you will find a picture of Jesus who is *the* Overcomer. "Be of good cheer; I have overcome the world" (John 16:33). Jesus has overcome—past tense. The devil couldn't tempt him, the law lovers couldn't silence him, Pilate couldn't fault him, death couldn't keep him, and the grave couldn't hold him. Jesus conquered death and he now sits at the right hand of God, bearing a name above every name.

Who is an overcomer? You are, because Jesus is an overcomer and "as he is, so are we in this world" (1 John 4:17). You cannot be one with the Lord and not be an overcomer any more than you can be one with the ocean and not be wet.

> You are from God, little children, and have overcome them; because greater is he who is in you than he who is in the world. (1 John 4:4)

This is not a promise of a future reality but a statement of present fact. You *have* overcome because Christ the Overcomer lives in you. It makes no difference whether you are an old saint or a brand new believer, you are an overcomer because Jesus makes you so.

You may say, "But I don't feel like an overcomer." In Christ, you are an overcomer nonetheless. When you came to the Lord he made you a new creation. He gave you his overcoming DNA and his overcoming Spirit. You are now an overcomer by nature. It's in your genes.

It is important to let this truth take root in your heart lest you be tempted into the sort of dead works that seduced the Ephesians. If you don't see yourself as an overcomer in Christ, you will think there are two classes of Christians: There are the super Christians who overcome and are rewarded with special crowns, and then there are the Christian riffraff who frankly don't deserve to be in the kingdom. This is a false dichotomy. We are *all* undeserving riffraff, and we are *all* qualified by grace. Because of Jesus every believer is a crown-wearing tree-of-life-munching overcomer.

Yet the Bible goes even further than this. "In all these things we are more than conquerors through him who loved us" (Rom. 8:37). The word for conqueror is the same word for overcomer. In Christ you are more than an overcomer, but what does that mean? A conqueror has to fight to get the victory, but we are more than conquerors because Christ has won the war. Because of Jesus, we don't have to fight. We simply stand on the victory that Christ has accomplished on our behalf. Jesus the Overcomer has done the hard work; our part is to receive the benefits and say, "Thank you, Lord!"

The identity of a conqueror comes from a conquered enemy, but we are *more than conquerors* through him who loved us. Our identity comes from our first love who loved us, and it is a better identity by far. You may say, "I'm a cancer survivor," or "I'm a recovering alcoholic." Perhaps you've battled with abuse, addiction, or anxiety, and by the grace of God you have conquered or are conquering those enemies. But those enemies don't define you because you are *more than a conqueror*. You are not a rape victim; you are a daughter of the Most High. You are not a struggling porn addict; you're a son of the King. You need to see yourself as God sees you, for it is only with a proper sense of identity—one grounded in God's love for us—that you can begin to overcome in life's trials.[14]

35

How do we overcome? Through faith in Jesus the Overcomer. In union with Christ, you are an overcomer by nature. You have nothing to prove. To see Christ's victory in your daily struggles means working out by faith that which the Lord has already accomplished.

> For whatever is born of God overcomes the world; and this is the victory that has overcome the world — our faith. Who is the one who overcomes the world, but he who believes that Jesus is the Son of God? (1 John 5:4–5)

Spiritual warfare for the Christian is less about shouting at the devil and more about believing that Jesus is Lord over whatever situation we face. Unbelief says we must engage the enemy and fight for the victory, but faith declares that Jesus has already won. Unbelief cowers before the name of the adversary, whether it's disease, debt, or depression. But faith exalts the Name that is above every name.

Revelation 2:7c …I will grant to eat of the tree of life which is in the Paradise of God.

What is the tree of life? Jesus is the Tree of Life who sustains those who feed on him.

When we think of the Tree of Life we naturally think of the tree in the Garden of Eden. But Anatolian Christians unfamiliar with the Old Testament would have pictured the sacred tree that once grew in the heart of the Artemision.[15]

The Temple of Artemis in Ephesus was built on the site of an ancient tree shrine. Surrounding the temple, to a distance of about 200 yards, was a wall. Those seeking refuge from prosecution could find sanctuary inside this wall. In this way the Artemision became known as a refuge and a place of salvation. In reality, it was a slum for criminals and gangsters. It was a cesspit populated by lowlifes who, in the words of Heraclitus the philosopher, were only fit to be drowned.[16]

Yet it was among these dregs of society that Paul's gospel took root and brought forth a harvest of righteousness. On the site of the sacred tree a new tree, the Tree of Life, flourished and grew.

Who eats of the Tree of Life? The believer. Those who wash their robes in the blood of the Lamb have the right to eat of the Tree of Life (Rev. 22:14).

When Jesus tells the Ephesians that only overcomers get the right to eat of the tree of life, he is not trying to rev them up or threaten them. He is giving them a wonderful affirmation of their position in Christ. It's a mistake to think of overcoming as some sort of admissions test. Jesus is not trying to keep people out of his kingdom; he's trying to get them in.

Where is the Paradise of God? Wherever Jesus is.

Jesus is speaking a language any Ephesian would have understood, for paradise is a Persian word and Ephesus was once a Persian city. The Ephesians tried to build a paradise inside the walls of the Artemision. Their experiment had failed, but the dream was there. The Ephesians longed for a sanctuary and that's what Jesus offers them. Against their parody of paradise, the real thing: a living tree and a true Paradise.

Jesus is talking about himself, for he is the Tree of Life in the Paradise of God. He is our refuge and the fortress of our salvation. He is our resting place and our longing fulfilled.[17]

What was Christ's message for the Ephesians? "I've seen how hard you guys are working and how you don't put up with bad teachers. But you're so busy that you don't have any have time for me. I offer you rest, but you prefer labor. You have put yourselves under all this pressure and have forgotten how much I love and desire your company. This is not good. You're falling apart and heading for burnout. Turn around and go back to the beginning when everything was simple—just you and me enjoying each other's company. Good times! Let's do that again. I am the Tree of Life. Allow me to nourish and sustain you. Make my love your resting place. When you're in Paradise why would you ever leave?"

What is Christ's message for us? Make yourself at home in God's love and never leave.

If you are worn out from doing the Lord's work, you can probably relate to the Ephesians. They were a hard-working bunch of believers, but they were dying on the inside. They were busy building, but their labor was in vain.

Why do we push ourselves past breaking point? It can happen because we've forgotten how much God loves us. We think we have to prove ourselves or come up with the goods, but none of this pressure is from the Lord.

You were made to receive your Father's love. Lose sight of your Father's love for you and you will lose your way. You'll fall from the secure place of grace into the realm of dead works. You'll become restless, insecure, and empty on the inside. You'll try to replace his love with lesser things.

If the Ephesians could leave the love of God, anyone can. But the good news is those who wander can come home again. If you have lost your first love, Jesus shows us the way back: Remember, repent (change your thinking), and do what you did at first. Go back to the place of your first love, when Jesus was your everything. Make every effort to enter his rest and let nothing move you.

I pray that you may have your roots and foundation in love, so that you, together with all God's people, may have the power to understand how broad and long, how high and deep, is Christ's love. Yes, may you come to know his love—although it can never be fully known—and so be completely filled with the very nature of God. (Ephesians 3:17b–19, GNB)

2. SMYRNA

And to the angel of the church in Smyrna write: The first and the last, who was dead, and has come to life, says this: "I know your tribulation and your poverty (but you are rich), and the blasphemy by those who say they are Jews and are not, but are a synagogue of Satan. Do not fear what you are about to suffer. Behold, the devil is about to cast some of you into prison, so that you will be tested, and you will have tribulation for ten days. Be faithful until death, and I will give you the crown of life. He who has an ear, let him hear what the Spirit says to the churches. He who overcomes will not be hurt by the second death." (Revelation 2:8–11)

Smyrna was located thirty-five miles up the coast from Ephesus at the head of an inlet now known as the Gulf of Izmir. Although Ephesus had bragging rights as the greatest city in the province, Smyrna, with its magnificent harbor, huge theatre, and thriving wine trade, was a strong rival.

First-century Smyrna was a beautiful city with fine temples and towers. The Greek orator Aelius Aristides, one of Smyrna's most distinguished residents, described the city as a statue with its feet in the sea, its middle parts in the foothills, and its head, crowned with great buildings on Mount Pagos behind.[1]

While Ephesus was known as the Gateway to Asia, Smyrna was the Ornament of Asia. As Ephesus was the home of the goddess Artemis, Smyrna had the crowned goddess Cybele. Smyrneans also worshipped Dionysus, the Greek god of wine, and in 195BC they created a cult to the goddess Roma, a personification of Rome.

Why did Smyrna get the second letter? An Ephesian would say it was because Smyrna was the second city and second best. A more plausible reason is that Smyrna was the next city up the road from Ephesus.

Revelation 2:8a And to the angel of the church in Smyrna write:

Who is the angel of the church? *See Revelation 2:1a on page 20.*

Who was the angel at Smyrna? A young man called Polycarp (69–155). Polycarp was trained and ordained by the Apostle John.[2] We don't actually know if Polycarp was bishop at the time of these letters, but since John died not many years after they were written, there's a fair chance that he was. Polycarp would have been around 26 years old when he received this letter from Jesus. (Remember, the letters to the churches were sent to the leaders of each church.) About 60 years later, he was burned at the stake. As we shall see, he wasn't the only Christian killed for his faith in Smyrna.

Polycarp of Smyrna

What is the meaning of the name Smyrna? Myrrh, which is also the name of a spice we associate with death.[3] (Myrrh was one of the spices used to prepare Christ's body for burial (John 19:39), and myrrh mixed with wine was also the last thing Jesus tasted before he died on the cross (Mark 15:23, John 19:30).)

This connection with the spice of death is interesting because the letter to the Smyrneans is about death. It's the shortest of the seven letters, yet death is mentioned three times in four verses. The bad news is that some of the saints are going to be put to death. The good news is that Jesus has been there, done that, and lived to tell the tale.

Revelation 2:8b The first and the last, who was dead, and has come to life, says this:

Who is the first and last? Jesus, the Lord of history.

Three times in the Old Testament God describes himself as the first and the last (Is. 41:4, 44:6, 48:12). In the New Testament, Jesus does the same thing (Rev. 1:8, 2:8, 22:13). Jesus is the Alpha and Omega, the beginning and the end. It is a title to inspire hope among those who are approaching the end of their lives.

Who was dead and has come to life? Not Dionysus. According to the religious myths acted out on the stages of Smyrna, the god Dionysus was killed and brought back to life by his father Zeus. This story was a fiction that hinted at a greater truth, namely, the death and resurrection of the Son of God. When Jesus introduces himself to the Smyrneans as the dead and resurrected One, he's saying, "I'm the Reality that is being caricatured in your city."

Who else died and came to life? The city of Smyrna. Smyrna was originally founded as a Greek colony. But six hundred years before Christ, the local Lydians sacked the city, and Greek-Smyrna ceased to exist. However, three hundred years later, the city was rebuilt, better than ever. The One who died and came to life is showing his knowledge of the local situation by making a direct and obvious connection with Smyrna's past. He's saying, "I know you. I know where you come from; I know where you're going."

What is the significance of this introduction? The saints in Smyrna were being persecuted, and some were about to be killed for their faith. This would have been a frightening prospect. The One who was dead and has come to life writes to encourage them with the fact of his resurrection. "Death may bury you, but I am death's foe. I have conquered the grave and I will raise you up."

> **Revelation 2:9a I know your tribulation and your poverty (but you are rich)…**

What is tribulation? Tribulation means trouble or pressure in the sense of being oppressed or crushed.[4] To use an Australian expression, the Smyrneans were under the pump. They were being pushed around, bullied, and abused.

What tribulation did the Smyrneans experience? The church in Smyrna was afflicted with two kinds of trouble: extreme poverty and slander (as we will see). Like John on Patmos, the Smyrneans were suffering for their faith in Christ.

What was the cause of this trouble? Religious Jews. Just as the Jews brought trouble to the apostles in Jerusalem and elsewhere, they agitated against the saints in Smyrna. The martyrdom of Polycarp in the second century and another saint called Pionius in the third testified to the "unusually virulent bitterness of the local Jewish community toward the Christians" in that city.[5]

Why were they impoverished? They had been mistreated and plundered.

Smyrna was a prosperous city, so why were the saints poor? The likely reason is they had been impoverished as a result of religious persecution. Perhaps their property had been seized or they had been shut out of jobs or they had lost money in frivolous lawsuits. Maybe their homes had been pillaged (see Heb. 10:34). Whatever the cause, the Smyrneans had been left destitute. They were the poorest Christians in Asia.

Poor yet rich? The Smyrneans had no money, yet they were heirs of all things in Christ.

> Listen, my beloved brethren: did not God choose the poor of this world to be rich in faith and heirs of the kingdom which he promised to those who love him? (James 2:5)

If the gospel is good news for anyone, it's good news for the poor and downtrodden. It's not that Jesus has anything against the rich and comfortable, as we will see when we get to wealthy Laodicea. It's just that the rich have a hard time receiving what the Lord wants to give them. Not so the poor. With empty hands they are more than ready to take what Jesus provides.

> For you know the grace of our Lord Jesus Christ, that though he was rich, yet for your sake he became poor, so that you through his poverty might become rich. (2 Corinthians 8:9)

How do the poor become rich? By being adopted into the family of God. He who is a joint heir with Christ is the heir of all things (Rev. 21:7). The Smyrneans, although they had nothing, had Christ, and he who has Christ has everything (Rom. 8:32). While they were poor in the eyes of the world, they were rich in faith and heirs of the kingdom.

Revelation 2:9b …and the blasphemy by those who say they are Jews and are not, but are a synagogue of Satan.

Who are the Jews that are not Jews? Religious Jews. Who else would claim to be a Jew but a Jew? But what is a Jew? According to the Apostle Paul, a true Jew is anyone who has been circumcised in the heart by God (Rom. 2:28–29). A believer, in other words, regardless of their race (Rom. 4:11). "They are not all Israel who are descended from Israel" (Rom. 9:6).

According to this definition, the religious Jews who persecuted Jesus and the apostles were not true Jews. In rejecting the faith of their father Abraham, as well as the testimony of the law and the prophets, they proved themselves false. "They say they are Jews but are not."[6]

Does Jesus hate the Jews? Far from it. Jesus loves all Jews! And so does John, the Jewish writer of these letters.

Jesus is not talking about Jewish people in general. He's describing fanatics who torture and kill in the name of religion. Think of the Pharisees who bayed for his crucifixion. Or the Sanhedrin who flogged the apostles and stoned Stephen (Acts 5:40, 7:58). Or the Jews who conspired with the chief priests and elders to kill Paul (Acts 23:12–15). These extremists were religious terrorists, the al-Qaeda of their day.

Who are the synagogue of Satan? Religious Jews who embraced a satanic agenda of violence and murder.

The Jews referred to themselves as the assembly of the Lord (Num. 16:3), but the Lord called them the assembly or synagogue of Satan. He was not referring to God-fearing Jews who revered the law, but religious fanatics who hated him and killed those who got in their way. "You are of your father the devil," said Jesus to the murderous Pharisees (John 8:44), and he's saying something similar here.

Religious Jews persecuted Jesus in Judea, and they persecuted his followers in Smyrna. One story will suffice: When Polycarp was brought to the stadium to be martyred, both Gentiles and Jews clamored for his death. Even though it meant breaking their Sabbath, the latter eagerly gathered the wood with which to burn him.[7]

Why bring Satan into this? Because Jesus doesn't want you to hate the Jews.

The religious Jews were on the wrong side of Jesus, but they were not the enemy. The true enemy is the one who has been opposed to all that is good and godly from the beginning.

> For our struggle is not against flesh and blood, but against the rulers, against the powers, against the world forces of this darkness, against the spiritual forces of wickedness in the heavenly places. (Ephesians 6:12)

When we are mistreated, the temptation is to take up arms against our oppressors. Instead of loving and praying for our enemies, we are inclined to smite them, perpetuating the cycle of violence. Jesus interrupts this destructive cycle by exposing our true enemy, which is Satan. He does not do this to elevate the devil as much as to save you from becoming his unwitting tool.

In these letters from Jesus, we encounter some wicked people: Nicolaitans in Ephesus and Pergamum, a seductress in Thyatira, and religious fanatics in Smyrna and Philadelphia. Jesus wants us to see past these misguided souls to the satanic origins of all enmity. We are not in a battle against people, but principalities and powers. It is not the Jewish synagogue that is crushing the church in Smyrna but the synagogue of Satan. It's not the Romans who are imprisoning the saints but the devil.

What blasphemy? The saints in Smyrna had been slandered by the religious Jews.

To blaspheme means to slander or falsely accuse. When Paul preached the gospel, religious Jews slandered him and his message (Acts 13:45, 18:4–6), and something similar was happening in Smyrna. The Jews were spreading lies about the church. They were saying things like, "Christians are opposed to Caesar. They're godless heretics who stir up trouble all over the world" (see Acts 17:6–7, 21:28).[8]

These lies were more serious than you might imagine, for they could draw the unwanted attention of the state. Indeed, this was the Jews' intent. To kill or imprison a Christian, all the religious Jews needed to do was spread slander or stir up civil unrest. Then they would stand aside and let the heavy-handed Romans deal with it (see Box 2.1).

44

Box 2.1: How to persecute Christians in a Roman world

Roman law forbade the practice of any religion other than the imperial cult. However, the Jews could purchase an exemption by paying the *Fiscus Judaicus* or Jewish tax. (This tax, which was imposed on Jews after the destruction of Jerusalem in AD70, was intended to replace the tithe that the Jews had formerly paid for the upkeep of the temple.) By paying the tax, the Jews were free to practice their religion. And by extension, so were the Christians.

To the Romans, the Christians were just another Jewish sect. As long as the Romans couldn't tell the difference, the Christians flew under the radar and enjoyed a measure of religious freedom. However, that freedom could quickly disappear whenever the Jews felt like picking a fight. We see examples of this in the New Testament.

In Corinth, the religious Jews brought Paul into the Roman courts on the charge of persuading men to worship God contrary to Jewish law (Acts 18:12–13). They basically said, "Paul is not one of us, therefore he is breaking Roman law." On that occasion the Roman proconsul did not take the bait. But there were times when the Jews played the Romans like fiddles. In Jerusalem, some Jews from Asia recognized Paul and started a riot. The Romans showed up and Paul ended up in chains and on trial for his life (Acts 21:27ff).

The Jews weren't the only ones who spread lies about the Christians. The pagan idol-worshippers, whose businesses were perpetually threatened by the liberating gospel of Jesus, also slandered the church. John Foxe, who compiled *Foxes' Book of Martyrs*, describes how the early Christians were slandered:

Such was the infatuation of the pagans, that, if famine, pestilence, or earthquakes afflicted any of the Roman provinces, it was laid upon the Christians. These persecutions among the Christians increased the number of informers and many, for the sake of gain, swore away the lives of the innocent.[9]

Why were the Jews hostile towards the Christians? Because some of the Jews had become Christians, and those who hadn't often hated those who did. The religious Jews would not have cared if converts had come from the pagan population, but to see "renegade Jews" turning to Christ aroused their hatred.[10]

Revelation 2:10a Do not fear what you are about to suffer.

What were they about to suffer? Imprisonment and death.

The Jesus of the Gospels warned his disciples that they would be handed over to the courts and hauled before officials for the sake of his Name (Matt. 10:17–18), and it's the same warning here. The saints in Smyrna were already suffering, but their troubles were about to get worse.

Do not fear?! How is it possible to not fear death? Because the Risen Lord has conquered the grave.

All die, but not all fear death. Death is inevitable, but fear is a choice. When you see Jesus who was dead but has come to life, faith rises and fear diminishes.

> Do not be afraid; I am the first and the last, and the living One; and I was dead, and behold, I am alive forevermore, and I have the keys of death and of Hades. (Revelation 1:17b–18)

Is "Do not fear" a command that must be obeyed? It's an invitation to walk by faith.

A law mindset interprets Christ's words as commands to be obeyed, but Jesus is dispensing grace. He's giving a timely word of encouragement.

Revelation 2:10b Behold, the devil is about to cast some of you into prison, so that you will be tested, and you will have tribulation for ten days.

The devil personally threw them in prison? More likely it was those doing his diabolical work, namely Roman officials prompted by Jews from the synagogue of Satan. But let us not despiritualize the Lord's words. The devil, not the Jews, was ultimately responsible for this crime. Those who do the devil's work are but lost souls in need of salvation, just like the rest of us.

When we go through trials and tribulations, the accuser of our souls may whisper, "This is God's judgment for your mistakes and failures." But Jesus would say, "Don't blame God for the devil's work. It is the thief who robs, steals, and kills." We are supposed to resist the devil (Jas. 4:7), but we won't if we think God is behind our suffering. We need this word of truth from Jesus if we are to overcome the accuser.

In what sense were they tested? The devil's intent was to test the saints' allegiance to Christ and force them to renounce the Lord. This test involved pressure from the state authorities, undeserved prison sentences, and in some cases torture and the threat of execution.

In Roman times, legal proceedings typically commenced with a loyalty oath. This oath was intended to test a citizen's allegiance to the emperor. Loyalty oaths had been used in Rome for hundreds of years and, within certain limits, Christians were happy to take them.[11] But an ill wind began to blow in the late first century when the ruthless Domitian ascended to the throne and began referring to himself as lord and god.[12] It was soon apparent that this was the honor he demanded from his subjects, and it is likely this label was used in oaths. This

The "lord god" Domitian

oath made life very difficult for the Christians. "If they refused to take it," said John Foxe, "death was pronounced against them; and if they confessed themselves Christians, the sentence was the same."[13]

Despite the threats imposed upon them, many Christians refused to take the oath. "I will not give the title of god to the emperor," said the second-century Christian author Tertullian.[14] Neither would Polycarp. On the day of his execution, he was offered freedom if he would but declare Caesar to be lord. Polycarp refused and was martyred.

What is tribulation? Trouble. *See Revelation 2:9a on page 41.*

What is the significance of ten days? The time of testing will be short.

Some have speculated that the ten days refers to ten periods of persecution or ten bad emperors, but the simplest interpretation is the best: Jesus is giving the saints some perspective to help them endure what is coming. Trials are temporary; eternity is forever. There will be trouble, but it will only be for a brief time.

Revelation 2:10c Be faithful until death, and I will give you the crown of life.

Who's faithful? Smyrna was faithful.

Among the Smyrneans, it was a matter of civic pride that their city had been among the first cities in the region to back an emerging power called Rome. While their neighbors were still testing the waters, Smyrna threw its lot in with Rome and its loyalty to the republic was highly regarded. Cicero the Roman statesman described Smyrna as "a city of our most faithful and most ancient allies."[15] The Smyrneans' fidelity was so fervent that it gave rise to the political cult of *Dea Roma*. The Smyrneans literally worshipped Rome.

Telling a Smyrnean to be faithful was like telling a fish to be wet. They were famously faithful, but in an unhealthy direction. Their loyalty was misplaced, for Rome would let them down. Their false god would minister persecution and death. Far better to put their faith in Jesus who crowns the dead with resurrection life.

Is Jesus saying they're going to be martyred? Yes, some of them are going to be executed. In Roman times criminals weren't imprisoned except as a preliminary stage to trial (e.g., Acts 12:1–4). Jesus is saying, "After ten days of prison, some of you will be put to death."

Jesus wants the saints at Smyrna to know that the coming trouble will last only a short time. Those who get through it will endure on his account, while those who don't survive will have the joy of meeting him face-to-face.

Smyrna was not the only church where the saints were persecuted for their faith, but no church suffered more. The believers were bullied into poverty, their reputations were besmirched, and some of them were burned at the stake. They

The Crown of Smyrna

paid the ultimate price. Jesus forewarned them to prepare them. He wanted them to know that he, not death, has the last word. "After death, life!"

What is the crown of life? Resurrection life.

When Lazarus died, Jesus comforted his sister Martha with a hope-filled promise. "I am the resurrection and the life; he who believes in me will live even if he dies" (John 11:25). Jesus echoes that promise here, and he does so in the language of his readers. "The Crown of Smyrna" was a well-known phrase among the Smyrneans. It referred to Mount Pagos and the circlet of buildings that rose above the city, a crown that "had been before their eyes and minds from childhood."[16] Crowns or garlands of flowers were also worn in the ritual worship of local idols. The Jesus who meets us where we are adopts yet another local reference to illustrate a gospel truth. "Let those fading crowns remind you of the lasting crown of life."

To receive the crown of life is to be resurrected to new life. Jesus is promising resurrection to believers who are about to be condemned to die. And since we are all condemned to die one way or another, this promise is for all of us. "If we have been united with him in a death like his, we will certainly also be united with him in a resurrection like his" (Rom. 6:5). What is the condition for a resurrection like Christ's? It's identifying with Christ's death. It's believing, "I have been crucified with Christ and I no longer live, but Christ lives in me…" (Gal. 2:20). Those who have died with Christ will be raised with Christ.

> Behold, I tell you a mystery; we will not all sleep, but we will all be changed, in a moment, in the twinkling of an eye, at the last trumpet; for the trumpet will sound, and the dead will be raised imperishable, and we will be changed. (1 Corinthians 15:51–52)

You became a brand new creation the moment you were placed in Christ, but your body is still subject to decay and death. You were made new, but your earth suit was not. The good news is that Jesus is in the business of making *all things* new. One day he will transform our lowly bodies "so that they will be like his glorious body" (Php. 3:21). For those who die before the Lord returns, this is called a resurrection.

Who gets the crown of life? Those who love Jesus.

> Blessed is a man who perseveres under trial, for once he has been approved, he will receive the crown of life which the Lord has promised *to those who love him.* (James 1:12, italics added)

The crown of life is given to those who love the Lord, regardless of what trials we face and how well we face them. Those who insist we must show ourselves approved to earn the crown, perhaps by putting on a brave face and saying positive things as our world crashes around us, forget that we have already been tested and approved in Christ (Rom. 16:10). He whom the Lord approves has nothing to prove.

Near the end of his life, the Apostle Paul said, "I have kept the faith and there is laid up for me the crown of righteousness" (2 Tim. 4:7). Paul did not earn this crown by being faithful. Rather the crown is given to all who long for Christ's appearing (see 2 Tim. 4:8). The crown of life is for those who love the Author of Life. The crown is for the children of the King.

What if I'm not faithful until death? Jesus remains faithful; you still get a crown.

A mind untouched by grace twists the promises of Jesus into tests that must be passed and commands that must be obeyed. "Jesus was faithful unto death; you'd better be faithful too." And in the richest traditions of the old covenant, proper behavior is incentivized with carrots and sticks. "Be faithful and you'll get a crown. Be unfaithful and you won't." This is surely bad news for the saint who stumbles at the eleventh hour.

Others point to the crowns given to champion athletes as though only some win the prize. "You have to be faithful to the end to qualify for the reward." This, too, is a graceless analogy for it puts the focus on you and your performance instead of Jesus and his.

The temptation to view life as a test comes naturally to those of us who have been raised in a world that glorifies achievement, but Jesus doesn't speak that language. He does not dispense gold stars or crowns for good performance, but he crowns the undeserving and justifies the sinner.

But what about this scripture that comes later in John's book?

He who overcomes will inherit these things, and I will be his God and he will be my son. But for the cowardly and unbelieving and abominable and murderers and immoral persons and sorcerers and idolaters and all liars, their part will be in the lake that burns with fire and brimstone, which is the second death. (Revelation 21:7–8)

This scripture has been used to terrorize the saints. "If someone put a gun to your head and said, 'Deny Jesus,' would you prove cowardly? If so, you're going to hell." God help us. Admissions made under duress carry no weight in a court of law, so why do we think a just God would take them seriously?[17]

The Apostle Paul famously kept the faith, but what if he hadn't? What if he had fallen at the final hurdle? What if he had folded under Roman pressure and renounced the Lord? He would still get a crown of life! We may disown the Lord, but he will never disown us because he cannot disown himself.

Eternal life is a *gift* of grace (John 17:2, Rom. 6:23). It is not a reward given to those who pass the torture test.

So why be faithful? It's the life-giving choice.

Box 2.2: What happened to Polycarp?

When Polycarp (69 – 155), the aged Bishop of Smyrna, was brought to the stadium to be slain before the crowds, a way of escape was offered to him. "What harm is there in saying, 'Lord Caesar', and sacrificing and saving your life?" said the captain of the police. Polycarp refused. A similar offer was made by the proconsul, and again Polycarp did not oblige. Finally, the magistrate pressed him. "Swear allegiance to Caesar, revile Christ, and I will release you." Polycarp replied, "Eighty and six years have I served him, and he never did me wrong, how then can I blaspheme my king who hath saved me?"[18]

The proconsul threatened Polycarp with wild beasts and fire, but the old bishop, according to the historian, was "filled with courage and joy, and his face was suffused with grace." "Why do you delay?" said Polycarp. "Do what you will." When his executioners came to nail him to the stake, Polycarp said, "Leave me thus; for he who hath given me strength to endure the fire, will also grant me strength to remain in the fire unmoved without being secured by you with nails."

Polycarp died a noble death and the temptation is to marvel at his fortitude. "What a guy! What a super-Christian." But it wasn't human courage that held the old man to the stake as the flames consumed his body. Polycarp endured by the supernatural grace of God.

The story goes that when the thugs came for Polycarp, they found him, "full of the grace of the Lord." The old man had been lying in bed, but he cheerfully got up and ordered a meal be prepared for those who had invaded his home. When they sat down to eat, he asked for permission to pray undisturbed for one hour, and his request was granted. After this he went willingly to his death.

What happened during that hour of prayer? Perhaps he read the short letter Jesus had sent him 60 years earlier – the 129 words we know as Revelation 2:8-11. We can only speculate, but it seems clear that Polycarp had an encounter with the Risen Lord, and in that revelation, he found the grace to face death. Like David among the ruins of Ziklag, he strengthened himself in the Lord – the Lord who was dead but has come to life.

The exhortation to be faithful found at the end of verse 10 is the counterpoint to "do not fear" at the start of that verse. Jesus is offering us a choice. You can be fearful or faithful, and faithful is better. Fearful is what you get when you lean on your own resources; faithful is what you are when you hold on to Jesus. Fix your eyes on the source of your suffering and you will fear. But see the Savior who died but lives forevermore, and you will endure. Polycarp made the latter choice and this is why he was able to endure a brutal death.

Revelation 2:11 He who has an ear, let him hear what the Spirit says to the churches. He who overcomes will not be hurt by the second death.

What does it mean to have an ear to hear? *See Revelation 2:7a on page 32.*

What does the Spirit say to the churches? *See Revelation 2:7a on page 32.*

Who overcomes? *See Revelation 2:7b on page 34.*

What is the second death? It's the one that comes after the first or physical death. It's the ultimate outcome for those who reject the gift of life (see John 5:40, 10:28).

According to rabbinical tradition, the second death refers to the ultimate extinction of the wicked. It's God's final punishment that follows the first or physical death. It is not difficult to imagine the religious Jews threatening the Christians with this fate. "The Romans will kill you and then God will end you." To this terrifying threat Jesus replies, "It's not going to happen."

Jesus is the Living One (Rev. 1:18) and those who have been united with him in his death shall live with him forever more. The hope of eternal life appears in the seven letters as a tree of life (Rev. 2:7), a crown of life (Rev. 2:10), and a book of life (Rev. 3:5). This is Jesus riffing on his best-known gospel promise: "For God so loved the world that he gave his one and only Son, that whoever believes in him (i.e., is an overcomer) shall not perish (in the second death) but have eternal life" (John 3:16).[19]

What was Christ's message for the Smyrneans? "Some of you are going to be mistreated on my account and some of you may die. Don't be afraid, but fix your eyes on me. I was dead but have come to life. We'll go through this trial together, and you'll be amazed at how well your God-given faith bears up under pressure. This test will only be for a short time and then we will meet face to face. I can't wait to see you and hug you and give you your crown."

What is Christ's message for us? Fear not, for Jesus is the resurrection and the life.

If you have received the sentence of death, perhaps in the form of a bad medical report or a lost opportunity, take heart: Death does not have the final word. The Alpha and Omega is the beginning and the end. The One who was raised to life invites you to see beyond that curtain to the realm of the everlasting. As a dearly loved child of the Most High, you have nothing to fear for nothing can separate you from his love. No matter how bad it gets, even if your heart stops beating and they bury your body in the ground, there is hope. Put your trust in Jesus for he will never let you go.

> Even though I walk through the valley of the shadow of death, I fear no evil, for you are with me. Your rod and your staff, they comfort me. You prepare a table before me in the presence of my enemies. You have anointed my head with oil; my cup overflows. Surely goodness and lovingkindness will follow me all the days of my life, and I will dwell in the house of the Lord forever. (Psalm 23:4–6)

3. PERGAMUM

And to the angel of the church in Pergamum write: The One who has the sharp two-edged sword says this: "I know where you dwell, where Satan's throne is; and you hold fast my name, and did not deny my faith even in the days of Antipas, my witness, my faithful one, who was killed among you, where Satan dwells. But I have a few things against you, because you have there some who hold the teaching of Balaam, who kept teaching Balak to put a stumbling block before the sons of Israel, to eat things sacrificed to idols and to commit acts of immorality. So you also have some who in the same way hold the teaching of the Nicolaitans. Therefore repent; or else I am coming to you quickly, and I will make war against them with the sword of my mouth. He who has an ear, let him hear what the Spirit says to the churches. To him who overcomes, to him I will give some of the hidden manna, and I will give him a white stone, and a new name written on the stone which no one knows but he who receives it." (Revelation 2:12–17)

The royal and ancient city of Pergamum was located 60 miles north of Smyrna and 15 miles inland from the Aegean Sea in the region of Aeolis. Pergamum was not as prosperous as Ephesus or Smyrna, but according to Pliny the Elder it was "by far the most famous city in Asia."[1] It was also the most powerful, for Pergamum was the seat of authority, a home of kings and conquerors. It had been the capital of the Kingdom of Pergamum before the Romans made it the capital of the Province of Asia.

Approaching first-century Pergamum, the first thing you would notice was a column of smoke rising from a flat-topped hill or mesa. Closer investigation would reveal the smoke as coming from the monumental altar in front of the Temple of Zeus. This temple, along with an older temple to Athena and another for Dionysus, formed part of a hilltop acropolis that dominated the town. Off to the side was a fourth temple for the imperial cult of Rome.

Lower down the hill were temples for the Pergamene god of Asclepius and the Egyptian god Serapsis as well as sanctuaries for the Greek gods Demeter and Hera. Pergamum was town of temples, a home to pagan cults both old and new.

Once upon a time, Pergamum had a world-class library. It had been built by King Eumenes II (197—159BC) to rival the great library at Alexandria. King Ptolemy of Egypt was miffed by the new library, so he banned the export of Alexandrian papyrus. No papyrus meant no new books, so Eumenes devised a method for writing on the untanned hides of sheep and goats. Apparently, he invented parchment.[2]

Whether parchment was actually invented or merely improved in Pergamum is open to debate, but the Latin word for parchment, *pergamenum*, is derived from the name of the city. Why does this matter? Because without parchment, the seven letters from Jesus would have been well and truly lost. If the earliest manuscripts had been recorded and copied onto papyri, they would not have survived. Indeed, without parchment we would have no Bible. You may be reading this book on paper or on a screen, but you would not be reading it at all if the clever Pergamenes hadn't figured out how to write on the skins of dead animals.

Revelation 2:12 And to the angel of the church in Pergamum write: The One who has the sharp two-edged sword says this:

Who is the angel of the church? *See Revelation 2:1a on page 20.*

What is the meaning of the name Pergamum? Pergamum means height or elevation, and this is a suitable appellation for a city that towered above others in power and authority.[3]

Pergamum represented the pinnacle of human advancement, for it was a city where men were worshipped as gods. Two hundred years before the birth of Christ, Attalus I assumed the titles of king and savior, while his son, Eumenes II of parchment fame, was revered as savior and god.[4] These self-made gods embodied the satanic desire to ascend to the highest place (Is. 14:12–14), and in Asia, there was no higher place than powerful Pergamum.

What's with the sharp, two-edged sword? Roman governors were divided into two ranks: those with swords and those without. Those with swords had been granted the *ius gladii*, or the right of the sword. This meant they held the power of life and death over those they governed. Since Pergamum was the capital of Asia, the ruling proconsul or regional governor would have worn a sword. He was effectively a mini-emperor with the power to punish those who refused to worship the emperor. In short, he could kill Christians.[5]

Why does Jesus have a sword? In Roman times, the sword or *gladius* was the symbol of absolute authority, and it is a Roman sword that Jesus has here. He's not holding an Oriental scimitar or a Greek *makhaira*, but a sharp double-sided sword such as a Roman governor would have. The letter to Pergamum is the only one that mentions Jesus with a sword because Pergamum was the seat of power.

What is the significance of this introduction? The Lord-with-a-sword is the Lord above all.

Pergamum had a long and bloody history of swordplay. It had been conquered by Greeks, Persians, Thracians, then more Greeks, before being given to the Romans and their sword-wielding governors. The Roman emperor ruled by the power of the sword, but the Lord-with-a-sword is the Lord of all and the true lord of Asia. The Romans, Goths, Sassanids, Byzantines, Seljuks, and all the other later rulers of Pergamum have come and gone, but the kingdom of the Lord endures and will never be destroyed.

Yet there is another reason why Jesus appears here with a sword. In the Gospels, Jesus said, "I did not come to bring peace, but a sword" (Matt. 10:34). He was referring to the sword of truth that sets a son against his father and a daughter against her mother. It's not that Jesus is in the business of wrecking families, but people divide themselves by their response to truth. Such a divide was forming in the church at Pergamum. A group called the Nicolaitans had introduced a destructive teaching and some were being led astray. So Jesus came to them with the sword of truth to slice through the lies and set them straight.

The Lord-with-a-sword was a powerful revelation for the power-conscious Pergamenes. It was also a great comfort for the oppressed believers. Jesus was saying, "Fear not, for your Protector is mightier than your oppressor. He who is for you is greater than he who is against you."

Revelation 2:13a I know where you dwell, where Satan's throne is...

Did Satan have a throne in Pergamum? Satan's throne is a reference to Rome and the imperial cult.

Pergamum, like other Asian cities, was home to many temples that extorted money from the gullible and credulous. What made Pergamum unique, however, was the concentration of religious and political power — power that increasingly opposed the gospel of Jesus Christ. In the time of the Apostle Paul, the most vigorous opposition to the church came from Jews and Judaizers. But in the latter years of John, the Imperial government of Rome had begun to assert itself as the Church's most dangerous enemy.

In one of the earliest pagan accounts of persecution, Pliny the Younger, a governor of the Roman province of Bithynia and Pontus from 110–113, said he tested Christians by demanding they offer incense and wine to an image of Caesar. Those who refused he executed. Why did the Romans kill Christians? Because the Christians were different and therefore dangerous and potentially seditious. In Roman eyes, they were godless atheists who refused to worship ancestral idols. They held unauthorized assemblies — a sure sign of trouble — and were apparently cannibals who ate the flesh of Christ and drank his blood. In refusing to bow to the emperor, they defied Rome itself.[6]

In persecuting Christians, Rome became a tool of Satan, and Pergamum was where Satan's agenda was most ruthlessly enforced. As the seat of Imperial rule in Asia and the home of the Imperial cult, it was the place where Satan appeared to be enthroned (see Box 3.1).

In Pergamum, the monster of Rome, to use Ramsay's striking description, had two horns: a civil administration run by the sword-wielding proconsul and the state religion of the Imperial cult.[7] These horns cast a shadow of death over all who refused to acknowledge Caesar as lord.

> **Revelation 2:13b ...you hold fast my name, and did not deny my faith even in the days of Antipas, my witness, my faithful one, who was killed among you, where Satan dwells.**

What does it mean to hold fast his name? The Pergamenes had a choice of hailing Domitian as lord god or Jesus. The Christians chose the latter. Whether in the courts or the imperial temple, the saints refused to worship anyone but Jesus, the true Lord of all.

Box 3.1: The Imperial Cult in Pergamum

Temples to the imperial cult were built in nearly every Asian city, but Pergamum was the first. The imperial cult entered Asia when Pergamum was granted the right to build a temple in 29BC.[8] Fast-forward to the time of the seven churches and the Roman Emperor Domitian was calling himself lord and god. This was a serious problem for Asian Christians who found themselves in Roman courts. If they refused to acknowledge the lordship of Domitian, they could be shipped off to Pergamum to face the Roman sword.

Who was Antipas? A Christian martyred in Pergamum. The Bible provides no further information about Antipas, but Jesus knows him by name. He calls him "my faithful witness," which is the same name the Lord uses to describe himself (see Rev. 1:5, 3:14). High praise indeed.

According to traditions observed by the Orthodox Church, Antipas was appointed by the Apostle John as the Bishop of Pergamum. By preaching the gospel, Antipas began to convince the Pergamenes to stop worshipping idols. The pagan priests rebuked Antipas for leading the people away from their ancestral gods. They demanded that he stop preaching about Jesus and join them in making sacrifices to their idols. But Antipas, held fast and…

> …calmly answered that he was not about to serve the demons that fled from him, a mere mortal. He said he worshiped the Lord Almighty, and he would continue to worship the Creator of all, with his only begotten Son, and the Holy Spirit.[9]

Enraged, the pagan priests seized Antipas and roasted him alive inside a bronze bull. At least, that's the legend. Nobody really knows much about Antipas other than he was "killed among you." He was not the only Christian martyred in Pergamum, but he was probably the first.[10]

Did not deny *my* faith? Even after Antipas was brutally murdered, the saints kept the faith. But note whose faith they kept. "You did not deny *my* faith," said Jesus. They held to the faith of Jesus.

Some people like to talk about their faith and their works, but in these letters Jesus keeps the focus on himself. He repeatedly refers to *my* name (Rev. 2:3, 13, 3:8), *my* faith (Rev. 2:13), *my* works (Rev. 2:26), *my* word (Rev. 3:8), and *my* patience (Rev. 3:10). This is where Jesus wants our attention — not on our faith but his. Our faith may waver and fail, but the good news is that we are justified on account of his faith. "We have believed in Jesus Christ, that we might be justified by *the faith of Christ*" (Gal. 2:16, KJV). This is the biblical order; God acts and we respond. We love because he first loved us, and we believe because Christ first believed in us. He is our supplier of faith, hope, and love.

Truly these letters give us a unique and wonderful revelation of Jesus. Nowhere else in scripture does Jesus talk about "my faith". It's a revelation that sustained the Pergamenes in one of the most oppressive cities in the world. If Antipas was faithful unto death, it was because he held to the name and faith of Jesus. Similarly, if we want to be found faithful in our hour of testing, we must keep our gaze fixed on Jesus. Put your brittle faith to his unbreakable faith and you will be faithful indeed.

Why does Jesus mention Satan twice? He wants us to know his true enemy.

Many preachers refuse to talk about Satan for fear of giving him unwarranted attention, but in these letters, Jesus refers to him several times. He does it so that we might not be unaware of the devil's schemes. "Any persecution you are facing is the devil's work, but don't fear him. I'm the one with the sword."

As the Antipas story reveals, the saints in Pergamum were persecuted for their faith. From where did this persecution originate? Remove Satan from the story and you might blame idol worshippers or "the clash of culture and politics." But Jesus wants us to know that his enemy has a name, and it's not Caesar or Balaam or Nicolaitan. Although such people may be the agents of evil, Satan is the source.

In Smyrna, Jesus said it would be the devil who imprisoned the saints (Rev. 2:10). Similarly, the persecution in Pergamum can be traced back to Satan. It will be worth keeping this in mind as we read on.

Revelation 2:14 But I have a few things against you, because you have there some who hold the teaching of Balaam, who kept teaching Balak to put a stumbling block before the sons of Israel, to eat things sacrificed to idols and to commit acts of immorality.

Does Jesus hold our sins against us? No. God is not sitting in heaven writing demerits next to your name every time you make a mistake. Love keeps no record of wrongs (1 Cor. 13:5). But love does not stay silent when we put ourselves in harm's way.

When Jesus says, "I have a few things against you," he's saying, "There is something we need to talk about." It's an act of love, not condemnation. "Because I love you we need to address this thing before you hurt yourself."

What is the teaching of Balaam? "It's okay to participate in idol feasts and commit acts of immorality."

The false prophet Balaam was hired by Balak, king of Moab, to prophesy curses over Israel. The Lord told him not to do it, but Balaam had shekel signs in his eyes. Although he did not curse Israel with his mouth, he manipulated the Israelites into cursing themselves by tempting them to sin. He did this by getting Moabite women to invite Israelite men to pagan festivals before seducing them into sexual immorality (Num. 25:1–3). On account of his deviousness, the name Balaam has become synonymous with greed and deception.[11]

Balaam did what he did because he loved the wages of wickedness (2 Pet. 2:15). Never mind that the angel of the Lord stood in his way with a flaming sword saying, "Your way is contrary to me" (Num. 22:32). Money was Balaam's god. Apparently some in Pergamum felt the same way. They participated in the pagan feasts or made sacrifices to Caesar because it was good for business. "They were experts in greed" (2 Pet. 2:14) who followed Balaam rather than Jesus.

Who held to the teaching of Balaam? The Balaam followers, or Balaamites, were false teachers who taught a similar message as Balaam. They certainly did not refer to themselves as Balaamites, for that would have given the game away. In first-century Asia, they called themselves Nicolaitans.

Revelation 2:15 So you also have some who in the same way hold the teaching of the Nicolaitans.

Who were the Nicolaitans? False teachers who taught grace as a license to sin. They were not confused Christians. They were libertines who infiltrated the church and introduced destructive heresies. They promised freedom, but were themselves slaves of depravity (2 Pet. 2:19).

False teachers and false apostles may seem like Biblical boogeymen, but they are Satan's principle means for attacking the church from within (see 2 Cor. 11:13–15). Left unchecked, they destroy churches and ruin lives. When John said, "Watch that you do not lose what we have accomplished that you may receive a full reward" (2 John 1:8), he was referring to smooth-talking deceivers who draw people to themselves and away from Jesus. Jude, the brother of James, offered a similar warning:

> For certain individuals whose condemnation was written about long ago have secretly slipped in among you. They are ungodly people, who pervert the grace of our God into a license for immorality and deny Jesus Christ our only Sovereign and Lord. (Jude 1:4, NIV)

The Nicolaitans elevated intellect above faith, and Self above Savior. In so doing they denied the lordship of Jesus and undermined the faith of the weak. The Nicolaitans are named in the letters to Ephesus and Pergamum and are not mentioned anywhere else in scripture. They may have taken their name from Nicolas, one of the seven deacons listed in Acts 6:5, but the evidence for this is unconvincing.[12]

What did the Nicolaitans teach? The same thing as Balaam: "It's okay to participate in idol feasts and commit acts of immorality."

The question of whether Christians could eat food sacrificed to idols was one of the biggest issues facing the New Testament church. The Jerusalem Council discussed it (Acts 15), Paul wrote entire chapters on it (1 Cor. 8–10), and Jesus rebuked people in two cities for encouraging it (Rev. 2:14, 20). But what exactly was happening? And what relevance does this have for us?

In the idol-worshipping cities of Asia, a great part of civic life revolved around the worship of local deities. Public meetings opened with prayers and offerings to the patron god of the town, and trade guilds held dinners in temples. Even something as innocuous as a private meal among friends would usually involve meat left over from a temple sacrifice. A Jewish Christian, having been raised to abhor such things, would never be tempted to participate in these activities. But a Gentile convert had been doing it his whole life. To him it was normal. He didn't know any other way to live.

What happened at these idol festivals? Demons were worshipped, lives were ruined, and people died.

First-century idol festivals were not cultural shows put on for the benefit of selfie-snapping tourists. They were debauched spectacles manifesting every sort of depravity known to man. They began with prayers to demons and degenerated into drunken orgies and violence. For instance, during the Dionysian feast of Katagogia, masked men would run through the streets cracking heads with clubs. These idol worshippers shed blood with religious fervor, killing innocent people at will. Timothy, the Bishop of Ephesus, apparently tried to stop one of these mobs and was beaten to death for interfering.[13]

The Romans did nothing to halt these savage and barbaric festivals. If anything, they industrialized the practice of killing people for fun. In the stadium and theatres of Pergamum, gladiatorial contests were a regular part of imperial cult festivals. For the entertainment of the populace, criminals fought to the death or were burned at the stake or torn apart by wild animals.[14]

Public games, as the Romans called them, had been staged in one form or another for hundreds of years. When Domitian became emperor, he introduced a number of cruel and sadistic innovations. He organized gladiatorial contests between women and dwarfs. He made people fight blindfolded. He hired games-masters whose job it was to whip reluctant fighters and discourage cheaters. (How did they discourage cheating? They prodded fallen warriors with red-hot pokers to see if they were faking, and those who laid still had their heads smashed with hammers.)

How many people were murdered for amusement in Pergamum? Nobody knows, but it would have been in the thousands.[15]

None of the Asian cities was a particularly pleasant place to live, but Pergamum was the place to avoid. If the devils of hell conspired to create a city that consumed its own citizens with bloodthirsty abandon, it is hard to imagine how they could have exceeded the unfettered depravity of the idolatrous Pergamenes.

Did the Nicolaitans really say these festivals were okay?! Yes. They not only encouraged Christians to participate, but they flaunted their so-called freedom by joining in with abandon. This is what Irenaeus, the early church father, had to say about those who took such liberties:

At every heathen festival celebrated in honor of the idols, these men are the first to assemble… Others of them yield themselves up to the lusts of the flesh with the utmost greediness, maintaining that carnal things should be allowed to the carnal nature, while spiritual things are provided for the spiritual. Some of them, moreover, are in the habit of defiling those women to whom they have taught the above doctrine… Others of them, too, openly and without a blush, having become passionately attached to certain women, seduce them away from their husbands…[16]

Irenaeus, a Nicolaitan nightmare

Why would any Christian attend these devilish festivals? It was expected of them.

Ancient idol festivals were hellish parties that dispensed death and disease. From our distant perspective, it's hard to imagine how anybody, Christian or otherwise, could possibly be tempted to participate in these horrendous spectacles. People went because they were superstitious and afraid, and this includes Christians who should have known better.

Imagine you are a stonecutter living in Pergamum. For most of your life you have attended idolatrous festivals. Your trade guild runs an annual feast to the god of stonecutting, and the town's administrators insist you offer a pinch of incense to Caesar. Since you met Jesus, you think nothing of idols — "They're just lumps of stone" — but if you don't participate in the ritual sacrifices, it will be bad for business. You could lose clients and be kicked out of the guild. Refuse to make the token sacrifice to Caesar and you could be martyred.

What do you do?

You read the letters from the Apostle Paul and are convicted. "The sacrifices of pagans are offered to demons, not to God. I don't want anything to do with demons." Then Antipas is murdered and your resolve weakens. "What if I'm killed for taking a stand?" Enter the Nicolaitans. "Relax. It's perfectly fine to attend these festivals. As the Apostle said, we're not under law but grace." Their message is appealing, but you can't help but wonder how the Apostle of Grace would respond. What would he say about the situation? If only someone could set up a meeting between the Nicolaitans and Paul to settle this issue once and for all. Someone did. (See Appendix 2: Apostle Paul vs the Nicolaitans.)

Why did Jesus hate the works of the Nicolaitans? Jesus told the Ephesians he hated the deeds of the Nicolaitans (Rev. 2:6), and a good question to ask is why. Commentators provide two unsatisfactory answers.

Some frame the issue as one of lawbreaking. "The lawless Nicolaitans were violating the Apostolic Decree passed by the Jerusalem Council forbidding the consumption of idol foods" (see Acts 15:29). Then why didn't Jesus say so? If the Nicolaitans were breaking the rules, why didn't he lay down the law? Jesus didn't mention the Apostolic Decree because there was no Apostolic Decree. The Jerusalem Council met to discuss whether the Gentile Christians should be circumcised and keep the Law of Moses. They did not reject the old law of circumcision only to replace it with new laws pertaining to idol feasts (Acts 15:20). We are under grace, not law.[17]

Others frame the Nicolaitan issue as one of spiritual compromise, as though Jesus was upset that his church was spiritually impure. "Compromise arouses the jealousy of the Lord and causes him to remove his hand of protection." The picture of Jesus as the jilted lover withdrawing in a huff is a horrendous distortion of God's character. Jesus is not insecure, and purity is not the price you must pay to earn his love. God's love has no price tags.

So what was the problem with the Nicolaitans? They put people in harm's way and promoted unbelief in the goodness of God.

The idol-industrial complex of Pergamum was a machine for carrying out Satan's dark agenda. From the Altar of Zeus to the humblest shrine, the city was geared towards the ruination of all who participated in the vile festivals. The Pergamenes were enslaved to the power of sin and death. God's plan for liberating them was the gospel of Jesus Christ. But the light of the gospel was being dimmed by an attitude of accommodation. The church, which was supposed to be an advertisement for the kingdom of heaven, was presenting a mixed message. Instead of offering a radical alternative to the devilish enterprise, some in the church were supporting it.

Why did Jesus hate the deeds of the Nicolaitans? He was not angry because they were breaking the rules or compromising his standards. He was angry because they were feeding God's children to the devil's machine.

Jesus and the Apostles encouraged people to put their faith in God, while the false apostles and the Nicolaitans discouraged them. They may not have said it in so many words, but their message was "God cannot be trusted. Secure your future by worshipping demons." The fruit of their mixed-up message was appalling: Instead of idol worshippers coming to the church to find grace and freedom, the Christians were going to the temples and kowtowing to demons. Instead of spending themselves on behalf of the hungry and oppressed, the saints were effectively subsidizing Satan.

The Ephesians hated what the Nicolaitans were doing, but the Pergamenes were ambivalent. They were so hung up on the "all things are lawful" part of Paul's message that they forgot that "not all things are beneficial" (1 Cor. 10:23). When it came to what the Nicolaitans were teaching, they had no boundaries. "They make a good point," said some. "I'm not so sure," said others. They debated and discussed but they drew no line in the sand. So Jesus drew one for them. "I hate it."

End of debate.

End of discussion.

Is there a modern-day example of Nicolaitan teaching? Wherever you have a false teacher preaching grace as a license to sin, you have a Nicolaitan. False grace messages come in many forms but are easily recognized by their tacit approval of sin, usually in the form of sexual immorality. Modern-day Nicolaitans quote scripture and make bold claims about freedom, but the fruit of their message is bondage and death.

Make no mistake, Jesus hates the false grace message, but it's important to understand why he hates it. He doesn't hate it because he's allergic to sinners or because he's keen for us to keep the rules. He hates it because it destroys those who buy into it and because it renders his church ineffective. He hates it because counterfeit grace is a doorway to captivity (see Box 3.2).

Revelation 2:16 Therefore repent; or else I am coming to you quickly, and I will make war against them with the sword of my mouth.

How do we repent? *See Revelation 2:5a on page 28.*

Who needs to repent? The Nicolaitans and those who had bought into their destructive message.

Did the whole church need to repent? No, because not all had gone astray. Jesus said only *some* held to the teaching of Balaam and the Nicolaitans. Only those who have gone the wrong way need to turn around.

What happens if they don't repent? The Lord will come and fight against *them*, not *you*.

It may help if we identify the two groups within this church. First, there were those who held fast to the name of Jesus (verse 13); then there were some who bought into the false teachings of the Nicolaitans (verses 14 and 15). So one letter for two groups: the faithful and the foolish, the steadfast and the strays.

And where did the ungodly Nicolaitans fit in? They were not part of the church, but they were "among you" (Jude 1:4). Like wolves in the sheepfold, they had infiltrated the assembly.

Jesus says I'm coming to *you* (the church) to make war against *them* (the Nicolaitans). If the foolish don't turn around, Jesus will contend with the false teachers who are leading them astray.

> **Box 3.2: The two doors**
>
> Jesus died to set us free, and in Christ we are free indeed. But there are two ways we can lose our freedom, two doors that lead to different prisons. The first door is called the Law Door. Open this door and you will find rules and regulations you must keep to be blessed. In the first century, this door led to Judaism and zealotry. In our time the law is packaged as the path to holiness or spiritual maturity. Make no mistake; the Law Door leads to bondage and death, for the law enflames sin.
>
> The second prison door is called License. This door is advertised as the opposite of Law — do what you will for there are no rules — but this is a deceptive claim. Liberty is promised, but enslavement is delivered. In the first century, license was promoted by Nicolaitans and libertines such as Jezebel of Thyatira. In our time, license is sold as the humanistic path to self-awareness. Make no mistake; the License Door leads to bondage and death, for sin always exacts a toll.
>
> The two doors are the same but different. One door puts price tags on the free grace of God; the other removes the price tags from sin. Each door presents a unique temptation that has seduced Christians since the time of the seven letters. Some, like the Laodiceans, have been tempted towards Law; others, such as the Pergamenes and Thyatirans, have been tempted towards License.
>
> The best way to avoid these dangerous doors is to choose the greater Door that leads to freedom and open spaces (see John 10:9).

Some take Christ's words as judgment against the church, but any swordplay will be against those who are deceiving his sheep. It's ludicrous to think that the One who would not condemn the woman caught in adultery would wage war against his own bride.

What's with the sword in his mouth? The image of Jesus waging war with the sword of his mouth is a classic Revelation depiction of the final judgment (Rev.

19:11–21). But Jesus is not talking about Judgment Day here. He's saying those who had bought into the false grace message need to quickly repent, or there would be consequences.

The urgency of Christ's message is plain. There's no need to discuss or debate the meaning of his words. The license-preachers are bad; Jesus is good; follow him. But what will happen if the foolish don't repent? What exactly does Jesus plan to do with his sword?

Is Jesus going to slay the false teachers? Despite what you may have heard, the answer is an emphatic no.

Some commentators say Jesus will kill the Nicolaitans and their followers with his sword. "Balaam was killed with a sword. What happened to Balaam will happen to them." Except it won't, for Jesus has no intention of killing those he died for. The kingdom of God is not advanced by running people through. The sword of his mouth is the word of the Spirit (Eph. 6:17). It's the word of truth that sets men free.

We must take care not to picture Jesus as a merciless Roman governor. Far better to let scripture inform our image of the Lord-with-a-sword.

In the Old Testament, an angel with a sword opposed Balaam on the way and the intent was to get Balaam's attention (Num. 22:31). It's the same thing here. Jesus loves the Nicolaitans. He hates their *deeds*, but he loves *them*. He went to the cross for them. He stands before them with a sword to get their attention. "Come to your senses and turn to God."

What is Jesus going to do to the Nicolaitans? He's going to combat their diabolical lies with the cold steel of truth. Remember, the true enemy in Pergamum was Satan (Rev. 2:13). It was Satan's message the Nicolaitans were preaching. But Satan is no match for the Lord-with-a-sword. Just as light defeats the darkness, God's truth would defeat the enemy's lies.

What is the solution to most of the world's problems? It is the gospel of Jesus Christ, and that is what is needed here. "I came into the world to testify to the truth," said Jesus to Pilate (John 18:37). But for some, the gospel is not enough. They want Jesus to slay slackers with his sword. It's a murderous image, yet one

I often encountered in my reading. Apparently the Jesus of Revelation is a sword-wielding slayer of sinners, wholly unlike the Jesus of the Gospels.

As if.

We need to renew our minds and read these scriptures through the lens of the cross. One way to do that is to ask, what would Jesus have done with the Nicolaitans if he had encountered them during his time on earth? There are only two possibilities. Either he would have treated them the way he treated all sinners (with love and mercy), or he would have rebuked them like Pharisees. It's the latter action that is implied here.

> Why do you put up with the Nicolaitans... Enough! Don't give in to them; I'll be with you soon. I'm fed up and about to cut them to pieces with my sword-sharp words. (Revelation 2:15–16, MSG)

Balaam ignored the angel with the sword and was ultimately cut to pieces by the Israelites. If the Balaamites of Pergamum ignore the Lord-with-a-sword, they can expect to feel the sharp edge of his words. They will get the same message that Jesus gave to the stubborn Pharisees: "Woe to you." He will speak to them the same way he speaks to Jezebel in his next letter (see Rev. 2:20–23).

The Pharisees invited people to walk through the Law Door while the Nicolaitans opened the License Door. Jesus, the Living Door, rebuked both.

What will happen if the Nicolaitans don't repent? Their deceptive influence will come to an end and they will become a minor historical footnote.

The Pergamum church was divided; some heeded the Nicolaitans; others didn't. There were arguments and strife, but the letter from Jesus would put an end to all that. Anyone who had been in two minds about the idol festivals now had a clear word from the Lord.

Antipas had resisted the idol worshippers and had been honored by Jesus; the Nicolaitans supported the idol trade and had been rebuked. The time of deception and double-mindedness was over. The Nicolaitans could repent or they could leave, but what they could no longer do was deceive the church.

Jesus had spoken.

Revelation 2:17 He who has an ear, let him hear what the Spirit says to the churches. To him who overcomes, to him I will give some of the hidden manna, and I will give him a white stone, and a new name written on the stone which no one knows but he who receives it.

What does it mean to have an ear to hear? *See Revelation 2:7a on page 32.*

What does the Spirit say to the churches? *See Revelation 2:7a on page 32.*

Who overcomes? *See Revelation 2:7b on page 34.*

What is the hidden manna? Jesus.

The manna that fell in the wilderness was called bread from heaven (Ex. 16:4). It pointed to Jesus, who is the Living Bread from heaven. The *hidden* manna may be an allusion to the manna placed inside the Ark of the Covenant. The meaning is this: He who overcomes (i.e., believes that Jesus is the Son of God) receives the hidden manna (Jesus himself). Jesus is saying, "I know you have been offered idol food from below, but those who partake of me enjoy living food from above."

What is the white stone? Some token of the Lord's favor. There may be no object in scripture that has been interpreted as widely as these mysterious white stones or *tesserae*. Do they signify acquittals, honors, food allowances, admission to feasts, status, rewards, protection, friendship, or other privileges? Did they fall from the sky as the rabbis believed or were they cultural artefacts? Take your pick.

What is the new name? Your new identity in Christ.

The new covenant is characterized by God making all things new (Rev. 21:5), and many of these new things are mentioned in the Book of Revelation. There is a new Jerusalem (Rev. 3:12), a new heaven and earth (Rev. 21:1), a new song (Rev. 14:3), and here in the letter to Pergamum we have a new name.

The new name speaks of our union with Christ. The moment you were put into Christ, his life and name become yours.

The new name also hints at our destiny. In the Bible, the Lord gave names to several people, and each new name was prophetic. Abram the childless became Abraham the father of many nations, while Sarai the barren became Sarah the mother of many nations (Gen. 17:5, 15–16).

A "name which no one knows but he who receives it" speaks of intimacy rather than secrecy.

Your new name comes from your heavenly Father who made you and knows you better than you know yourself. Only your Father knows what he has written into your DNA. The adventure of your life is figuring out your new name and discovering the person God made you to be.

Why were the Pergamenes offered a new name? The promise of a new name had special relevance for Pergamum on account of one of the temples atop that smoky hill.

When Octavian became the de facto emperor of Rome, he was given a new name: *Divi Filius Augustus* (literally, "God's son, the increaser"). The new name signified a man divinely empowered and set apart to rule. In Pergamum, a temple was built in honor of that new name. It was a permanent reminder that a mere man could be exalted to the status of a god. Of course, that new name was a sham—Octavian was hardly the son of God—but any believer who refused to pay homage at the temple of the new name paid a price. A Roman with a sword could end their life. In view of this threat, the Lord-with-a-sword makes a wonderful promise. "Believe in me and I will give you a new name and a new life that no Roman can end." For those who refused to bow to idols or men and who faced the prospect of being murdered for their faith, this was a comforting promise indeed.

Are these rewards for overcoming behavior? No. The blessings represented by the manna, stone, and the new name come to every believer through grace alone.

Some say the Ephesians got to eat of the tree of life and the Pergamenes got to partake of the hidden manna because they did not eat idol food. Because they abstained from what was forbidden, they earned heavenly rewards. This is dead religion. You are not qualified or disqualified by what you eat. "Food will not commend us to God" (1 Cor. 8:8). In the economy of grace, we are not rewarded for what we do, but for what Christ has done. Every blessing comes to us through him alone (Eph. 1:3). There are no bonus blessings reserved for those who abstain from idol food.

What was Christ's message for the Pergamenes? "I know you folks are going through hell in Pergamum, especially my guy Antipas who was murdered. I know it seems like Satan rules your town, but I'm the one holding the sharp sword.

You have held fast to my name and not bowed to Caesar, but beware this Nicolaitan teaching that says it's okay to participate in idol feasts. These Balaam followers promise freedom but enslave all who heed them. I hate what they are doing. If you've bought into their false grace message, repent. Quickly turn around, otherwise I will come and deal with them the same way I deal with all grace killers—by letting them feel the sharp edge of my words! Forget that lousy idol food and feed on the bread of heaven. These idols and self-proclaimed gods offer misery and death. I'm offering divine life to all who trust in me."

What is Christ's message for us? When we find ourselves bullied and pushed around by life, we need a revelation of the Lord-with-a-sword. If the Lord-with-a-sword is for you, who can be against you (see Rom. 8:31–34)? The powerful may oppress you, even take your life. But the Lord-with-a-sword shall deliver you, even from the grave.

The sword of the Lord is for your protection, not your punishment. If you stumble and fall, Jesus defends you; he doesn't accuse you (1 John 2:1).

Yet some take this good news as a license to sin. They say sinning is okay because God's grace will cover any error. This is toxic teaching. God's grace is indeed greater than your sin, but sin can ruin your life. Steer clear of those who preach a licentious message lest you lose the freedom that Christ has dearly bought.

From time to time we have to make difficult choices: Do we become all things to all men or do we take a stand? Do we join in or remain apart?

When sin is involved and people are getting hurt, the choice is easy. God has called us to shine in a dark world, so shine, and have nothing to do with the deeds of darkness.

Jesus has given you a new name and a new identity. Your name is not sinner and your identity is not defined by your imperfect performance. You are a dearly loved child of God, so act like it. Be who God made you to be. Living from your God-given identity is the most rewarding life of all. Why would anyone eat the junk food of earth when they can feast on the heavenly manna?

Do not fear, for I have redeemed you; I have called you by name; you are mine! When you pass through the waters, I will be with you; and through the rivers, they will not overflow you. When you walk through the fire, you will not be scorched, nor will the flame burn you. For I am the Lord your God, the Holy One of Israel, your Savior. (Isaiah 43:1b–3)

4. THYATIRA

And to the angel of the church in Thyatira write: The Son of God, who has eyes like a flame of fire, and his feet are like burnished bronze, says this: "I know your deeds, and your love and faith and service and perseverance, and that your deeds of late are greater than at first. But I have this against you, that you tolerate the woman Jezebel, who calls herself a prophetess, and she teaches and leads my bond-servants astray so that they commit acts of immorality and eat things sacrificed to idols. I gave her time to repent, and she does not want to repent of her immorality. Behold, I will throw her on a bed of sickness, and those who commit adultery with her into great tribulation, unless they repent of her deeds. And I will kill her children with pestilence, and all the churches will know that I am he who searches the minds and hearts; and I will give to each one of you according to your deeds. But I say to you, the rest who are in Thyatira, who do not hold this teaching, who have not known the deep things of Satan, as they call them — I place no other burden on you. Nevertheless what you have, hold fast until I come. He who overcomes, and he who keeps my deeds until the end, to him I will give authority over the nations; and he shall rule them with a rod of iron, as the vessels of the potter are broken to pieces, as I also have received authority from my Father; and I will give him the morning star. He who has an ear, let him hear what the Spirit says to the churches." (Revelation 2:18–29)

Having gone north and along the coast, our tour of Asian cities now heads inland. Thirty-five miles down the road from Pergamum, we come to the Macedonian colony and garrison town of Thyatira. At first glance, you might think there was nothing special about this town. Pliny the Elder dismissed Thyatira as a city of no great importance.[1] It had no palaces, no universities, and no temple to Caesar. But Thyatira was famous for one thing: dye. This was the place to buy colored clothing, and purple clothing in particular.

In ancient times, purple dye was a costly substance harvested from shellfish. But a cheaper substitute, now known as Turkish red, could be made from the root of the madder plant. It was this more affordable type of purple that came from Thyatira.

Thyatiran dye provides us with a clue as to how the gospel may have come to this town. In Philippi, another Macedonian colony, the Apostle Paul met a Thyatiran merchant who traded in purple cloth (Acts 16:14). Her name was Lydia, and it was possibly she who brought the gospel back to her hometown. It could have been Lydia who planted the Thyatiran church we read about in Revelation.

Revelation 2:18 And to the angel of the church in Thyatira write: The Son of God, who has eyes like a flame of fire, and his feet are like burnished bronze, says this:

Who is the angel of the church? *See Revelation 2:1a on page 20.*

What is the meaning of the name Thyatira? Thyatira is probably a Lydian name, the meaning of which has been lost to history. However, Roswell Hitchcock, in his classic dictionary of scriptural names, interprets Thyatira as perfume.[2] It's a sweet-smelling name for a church that was the fragrance of Christ to those who were lost.

Who is the Son of God with eyes aflame? Not Apollo the so-called sun god.
The principal deity of Thyatira was Apollo, the son of Zeus.[3] Apollo Tyrimnaeus, to give him his Macedonian name, was probably introduced by Greek-speaking colonists. Yet this idol, like all the others, would be upstaged by the real thing. The son of Zeus was nothing compared to the true Son of God.

What's with those burning eyes? The Lord's burning eyes search hearts and minds (Rev. 2:23). They penetrate masks and charades. No motive or agenda is concealed from Jesus. Nothing is hidden from his sight (Heb. 4:13).

And the bronze feet? These are the glorious feet under which all things have been placed (1 Cor. 15:27). These are the feet of him who tramples upon his enemies (Ps. 60:12).

What is the significance of this introduction? Jesus is pulling rank and he's doing so in a rather unusual way. At no other place in the Bible does Jesus introduce himself as the Son of God. (He certainly infers it on a couple of occasions.

But normally Jesus prefers to call himself the Son of Man.) We've met Jesus with the lamps and Jesus with a sword, but this is *Jesus as God*. He's rolled back the heavens to reveal his most exalted name. "I am God's Son." Why such a weighty and glorious introduction? Jesus is establishing his divine authority as a preface to the harsh words he is about to unleash on a certain person. The Lord with blazing eyes has come to expose a dangerous charlatan, and this is happy news for Thyatira, as we shall see.

Revelation 2:19a I know your deeds, and your love and faith and service and perseverance...

What deeds does Jesus know? Jesus begins five of his seven letters by saying, "I know your deeds." He exhorts the Ephesians to do the deeds they did at first (Rev. 2:5); he rebukes the Sardians for having incomplete deeds (Rev. 3:2); and he promises to reward the Thyatirans according to their deeds (Rev. 2:23). Clearly our deeds or works matter to Jesus. But what sort of deeds is Jesus referring to?

The law preacher says, "Jesus is referring to our law-keeping performance. We must keep the commands to please the Lord." A similar interpretation is offered by the works preacher. "Jesus is saying we need to work out our salvation, do the deeds that prove our repentance, and pursue the spiritual disciplines." Both interpretations raise uncomfortable questions: How many deeds are needed to qualify? What if I neglect to keep all the commands? Worse, both interpretations do nothing but promote dead works and pride.

What are dead works? We can distinguish dead works from faith works. Dead works of the flesh lead to death, while faith works release abundant life. The former relies on self; the latter leans on the Spirit.

Living under any form of law is a dead work because the law is not of faith, and its purpose is to minister death (2 Cor. 3:7, Gal. 3:12). To insist we must keep the law of the old covenant or the commands of the new is to preach dead works. Such a message will inflame sin, minister condemnation, and leave you wretched.

Any works done to prove our salvation or complete our sanctification are also dead works because they reveal unbelief in the finished work of the cross. You don't have to finish what Jesus started for you are complete in Christ (Col. 2:10).

In him you are as saved and sanctified as you ever will be. Since the Author and Finisher of our faith has perfected us (Heb. 10:14), there is nothing you can do to improve upon what he has done.

Repenting from dead works and having faith in God is one of the elementary teachings about Christ (Heb. 6:1), yet many haven't grasped it. They're trying to keep the law or make themselves holy, and they are exhausting themselves. Their dead works are killing them. They have forgotten that in the kingdom, all is grace, and "if it is by grace, it is no longer on the basis of works, otherwise grace is no longer grace" (Rom. 11:6).

What are faith works? Faith works are what lovers do.

The word love appears four times in the seven letters and on three of those occasions, Jesus is referring to *his* love. To the Ephesians, Philadelphians, and Laodiceans, Jesus spoke of his love, but the Thyatirans were known for *their* love. "I know your love," said Jesus. And since the word for love is the divine *agape*, it wasn't really their love but God's love shining through them. This was a church that knew the love of God and was actively sharing that love with others.

It's important to establish the proper order. It is not our love, faith and service that impresses the Lord. Rather, we become commendable when we are impressed by *his* love, faith, and service. Jesus commended the Pergamenes for not denying his faith, and it's a similar story here. "I smell *agape* love," Jesus is saying. "You have received the love of my Father, you are giving it away, and that's a wonderful thing."

Some might say, "Love is a verb. We reveal our love by what we do." But the scriptures declare that *agape* love is a noun. Indeed, love is a Person, for God is love (1 John 4:8).

Love is not something to manufacture but receive, and those who receive the wild and uncontainable love of God can't help but give it away. This is a radical revelation for many, yet this was Thyatira's testimony. They were giving away what God had given them—which is heaven's recipe for changing the world.

What deeds matter to Jesus? The only work that counts is faith expressing itself through love (Gal. 5:6).

Every one of us has deeds of one sort or another. We should not be impressed that the Revelation churches had deeds, but we should ask, what sort of deeds were they? Were they dead works or faith works?

Jesus acknowledged the deeds of five churches, but only the Thyatirans' deeds bore the unmistakable marks of God's love and grace.

Revelation 2:19b …and that your deeds of late are greater than at first.

What are the later, greater deeds? The Thyatirans were growing in the grace and knowledge of Jesus and becoming increasingly fruitful.

Growing in the grace of God is not a sure thing. Many Christians start strong in grace before getting seduced into dead works. They hear about rules they need to keep (e.g., the Galatians), or they get distracted and wander from their first love (e.g., the Ephesians). Not the Thyatirans. They started well and continued in the faith.

How do we grow in grace? We grow as we discover more of the goodness of God and Jesus his Son. This is what the Thyatirans did. They made knowing Jesus their main occupation (see 2 Pet. 1:2). They kept their eyes fixed on the Lord and refused to be distracted from the main thing.

How does grace make us fruitful? As we grow in the grace and knowledge of Jesus, we bear his fruit naturally.

Some say that growth is the result of diligent study and personal discipline, but growth is a natural process. Growth is what happens when you feed on the goodness of God.

When you grasp how much your heavenly Father loves you, it gives you confidence to take risks. The dreams hidden inside you come to life and take wing. You fulfill your God-given destiny.

"Later, greater deeds" does not mean upping your output and working harder than ever. In fact, the pressure to do more for the Lord can leave you busy and barren. But the mystery of God's grace is that it empowers us to do far more than we could have ever accomplished on our own.

By the grace of God I am what I am, and his grace to me was not without effect. No, I worked harder than all of them — yet not I, but the grace of God that was with me. (1 Corinthians 15:10, NIV)

No one understood grace better than Paul, and no one worked harder. Similarly, no church in Asia understood grace better than the Thyatirans, and no other church was acknowledged for doing more than when they started.

Perhaps you have heard that Thyatira was one of the bad churches of Revelation. Many theologians dismiss the church as the most corrupt of the seven. It was anything but. True, it had some issues that Jesus is about to get to. But it was a fruitful church known in heaven for its love, faith, and service. It was the only church whose later deeds were greater than their first.

Revelation 2:20a But I have this against you, that you tolerate the woman Jezebel, who calls herself a prophetess, and she teaches and leads...

Does Jesus hold things against us? *See Revelation 2:14 on page 61.*

Who was Jezebel? She was Trouble. Some say she was the pastor's wife, but there is no evidence to support this. Others have speculated that she was Lydia, the possible founder of the church, but this is even more unlikely.[4] Still others have suggested she wasn't a person at all, but a metaphor for corrupt institutions or the apostate church. During the Reformation, some believed that Jezebel stood for the Roman Catholic Church. Today there are some who believe Jezebel represents those churches that preach a prosperity gospel or advocate same-sex marriages.

These are provocative speculations, but the simplest explanation is the most likely: Jesus was speaking about a real person who was both a false prophet (like Balaam) and a false teacher (like the Nicolaitans). False teachers are bad enough, but one that prophesies is particularly dangerous because her gifting lends credibility to her corrupting message.

Was she really a prophetess? She claimed to be so, but Jezebel was no prophet of God. She was a fake, an imposter. To quote Archbishop Trench, her prophetic inspiration was "such as reached her from beneath, not such as descended on her from above."[5] She operated in the counterfeit like the fortune-telling slave of Philippi (Acts 16:16). Bad prophecies plus bad teaching equals a bad influence on the Thyatiran church.

Was her name really Jezebel? Her name was likely metaphorical.

The original Jezebel was the most evil woman in the Bible. She was an idol-worshipping pagan who corrupted her Israelite husband, King Ahab, along with much of the nation (see 2 Kings 9–10). Jezebel encouraged the worship of Baal (think child sacrifices, murder, and bondage), massacred the Lord's prophets and intimidated the socks off Elijah. When her husband died, she effectively ruled the country as a tyrant for ten dark years.

The name Jezebel became synonymous with seduction, idolatry, and death. So when Jesus-with-burning-eyes uses this name to describe the false prophetess in Thyatira, he is using the strongest possible language to say, "Beware this woman!"

Was she a Christian? Definitely not. By giving her the worst name in history, Jesus leaves us in no doubt that this woman was far from God. Her fruit revealed that she was a false prophet according to the False Prophet Checklist of 2 Peter 2: She was captive to sin; she followed the way of Balaam; and her eyes were full of adultery. Jezebel was no confused Christian. She was a snake in the garden undermining God's word. She had to be stopped.

If she wasn't a Christian, how did she get in the church? Through the front door.

We should not conclude that Jezebel was a Christian merely because she went to church. Neither should we think that the Thyatirans made a mistake letting a sinner in the door. The church is for sinners and imperfect people.

So what was the problem in Thyatira? The church allowed a false prophet to teach a destructive message. The old story of King Ahab and Queen Jezebel reveals the damage that can be done when God's people fail to confront a domineering personality. In Thyatira, the church tolerated a false prophet and some of the Christians were led astray.

Why did they tolerate her? We can only speculate. Maybe they were intimidated in the same way that Elijah was intimidated by the original Jezebel. Maybe they were afraid of her. But Jesus wasn't. The Son of God with blazing eyes would deal with this wicked Jezebel.

> **Revelation 2:20b ...she teaches and leads my bond-servants astray so that they commit acts of immorality and eat things sacrificed to idols.**

What did Jezebel do? She seduced Christians into adultery. Like Balaam, she led God's people into idol worship and sexual immorality.

Wasn't her immorality merely metaphorical? The King James Bible says she "seduces my servants to commit fornication," and in the Bible fornication sometimes means *spiritual* fornication. Running back to the law or worshipping idols is essentially cheating on Jesus. But the context here suggests Jezebel was promoting the sort of sexual immorality that was practiced at pagan temples and idol feasts.

Idol feasts were a problem for the saints in Pergamum, but they were an even bigger problem in Thyatira. This was because the town had an unusually large number of trade guilds. There were guilds for dyers, wool workers, linen workers, leather workers, tanners, potters, bakers, bronzesmiths, and slave dealers. If you wanted to work in Thyatira, you had to join one of these guilds. This put Christians in a difficult position since the guilds ate shared meals in temples. These feasts began and ended with sacrifices to idols and were characterized by drunken revelry and sexual immorality.

A Christian who refused to participate in the ceremonies of a guild was, in the words of William Barclay, "committing commercial suicide."[6] Unable to work, he would soon be faced with poverty and hardship. In Pergamum the Christian's *life* was threatened by the imperial cult, but in Thyatira his *livelihood* was at stake.[7]

How did the Christians survive? They flipped burgers. They took on low-skilled jobs that kept them out of the guilds but barely put food on the table. They went without. Then Jezebel began preaching her licentious message: "God

82

doesn't want you to starve, so go ahead and join those guilds. Have the freedom to participate in the idolatrous feasts and sleep with temple prostitutes."

Did Jezebel preach the same message as the Nicolaitans? Essentially, yes, but with more emphasis on sex. In Pergamum the Nicolaitans enticed the people to "eat things sacrificed to idols and commit sexual immorality" (see Rev. 2:14), but with Jezebel the order was reversed. "She misleads my servants into sexual immorality and the eating of food sacrificed to idols," said Jesus. This suggests that sexual immorality was a bigger concern in Thyatira.

In first-century Asia, idol worship was synonymous with sexual promiscuity. Fertility rites, temple prostitution, and orgiastic displays were an inherent part of pagan ceremonies. Fornication was common, while chastity was an unheard-of virtue practiced only by Christians.[8]

"Flee from sexual immorality," said the Apostle Paul (1 Cor. 6:18), but Jezebel embraced it. Unlike Joseph who ran from temptation, she ran towards it. The promiscuous prophetess considered herself free from all restraint, and she promoted pagan immorality.

Some Bibles say, "She teaches and leads my servants astray." A better translation is, "She teaches *and seduces* my servants." Jezebel was a seductress and a temptress who led Christians into sexual immorality. Through her teaching and influence she wrecked marriages and destroyed families, yet the Thyatirans did nothing. They tolerated her. So Jesus showed up like a husband confronting a Lothario hitting on his wife. This was not Jesus meek and mild. This was the Son of God incandescent with righteous fury. "Stop messing with my church!"

Revelation 2:21 I gave her time to repent, and she does not want to repent of her immorality.

Why did Jesus not show grace to Jezebel? He did! He gave her time to repent.

Under the Law of Moses, adulterers, fornicators and idol worshippers were put to death straightaway (Deu. 17:5). Had Jezebel lived in ancient Israel, her life would have come to a swift and violent end. But Jesus gave Jezebel grace. He gave her life when the law demanded death.

"I gave her time to repent," says Jesus.

This suggests that Jezebel had been warned at least once before. Someone had confronted her. (Was it John? Lydia?) But she didn't listen.

Jesus adds that she doesn't even *want* to repent. She loves her illicit lifestyle much as Balaam loved the wages of wickedness. She's no naïf caught up in the wrong crowd. She's in a bad place because she wants to be.

Does grace come with an expiry date? As long as there is life, there is hope, but there was little hope for Jezebel. It's not that Jesus was fed up with her, but by yielding to sin again and again, she lost her ability to choose. The lies she told herself robbed her conscience of the capacity for truth. By hardening herself to the grace of God, she put herself beyond repentance (Heb. 6:4–6).

Revelation 2:22a Behold, I will throw her on a bed of sickness...

Is Jesus going to make her sick? If she gets sick, Jesus won't be the one making her sick. Jesus cannot give what he does not have, and he has no sickness. When he walked the earth, Jesus never gave sickness to anyone.

But he's going to kill her, right? No. Jesus is the Author of life, not the angel of death.

It's true that some have used to verse to frighten people. "If you don't stop sinning, Jesus is going to take your life." But Jesus made no such threat. To do so would be contrary to his character and mission. Jesus doesn't want Jezebel, or anyone, to die; he wants her to repent. The Lord "is patient with you, *not wanting anyone to perish*, but everyone to come to repentance" (2 Pet. 3:9). Since Jezebel doesn't want to repent, death is a real possibility. But Jesus is not going to kill her. He is not going to pick up rocks like an angry Pharisee. Death is sin's wage.

So what exactly is Jesus going to do to her? He's going to oppose her, and he's already started.

Jezebel's fundamental problem was pride. By elevating her understanding above the word of God, she set herself up for a Luciferian fall. God gives grace to the humble, but he resists the proud. This is not done out of punishment, as though God were gracious one minute and punitive the next. The One who sits on a throne of grace is gracious through and through. God resists the proud so that they may see their need for grace.

What does it mean to be cast on a bed of suffering? She's going to reap what she has sown in accordance with the Lord's ancient design.

The Maker of heaven and earth created a world where actions have consequences. "If you eat from the tree you shall surely die," said God to Adam. Adam ate and Adam died, and it was all his own fault. God didn't kill him, but he made a universe where choices have consequences. That's what Jesus is talking about here. Jezebel has resisted the Lord so he will resist her. But his resistance will not come in the form of fire from heaven or anything like that. The consequences of Jezebel's actions will be more prosaic and connected to her misdeeds.

Let us be clear: Jesus is not about to punish Jezebel. How could he when he had already borne all the punishment for her sin on the cross? However, the Lord-with-eyes-aflame will oppose her and her false ministry and the result is she will be taken down. In rejecting the good news, Jezebel opted for bad news, and that's what Jesus gives her.[9]

Why a bed of suffering? Because it was in the bedroom of her immorality that Jezebel sowed a sinful seed. Perhaps she thought her actions would have no bitter consequences. If so, she was tragically mistaken. Fool around with multiple partners at temple orgies frequented by diseased pilgrims and it won't be long before you end up in a bed of sickness. It's practically inevitable.[10]

Why doesn't Jesus just say, "You're going to get sick"? Because Jesus is no mere fortune teller foretelling the consequences of Jezebel's sin; he is the Son of God speaking to edify his church.

The three most important words in this letter are found at the start of this verse: "Behold, I will…"

To a church that did nothing, Jesus is saying, "Watch, I am going to do something." It's a thrilling promise for a church that didn't know what to do.

The Thyatirans were like Elijah who did nothing about the first Jezebel. Elijah was intimidated by the tyrant queen and ran away frightened (1 Kings. 19:1–4). When the Lord caught up with Elijah he said, "Go anoint your successor."

Perhaps the Thyatiran Christians were ashamed of their inaction. Perhaps they were afraid that the Lord would rebuke them. If so, their fears were unfounded. In his letter to them there's no hint of the Lord's displeasure, only a wonderful promise. "You have done nothing about her. Behold, I will."

Why does Jesus speak so harshly to Jezebel? Because she's hurting people and destroying families. Just as the original Jezebel brought great suffering to Israel, this Jezebel was harming the people of Thyatira. By promoting adultery and idolatry, she was making people captive to sin.

The church is meant to be an embassy for heaven, but she was an ambassador for hell. While some were actively sharing the love of God, she was poisoning the well.

In his letter to Pergamum, Jesus threatened to wage war with the sword of his mouth on the Nicolaitans. What would such a war look like? We get a glimpse here in the letter to Thyatira, and it's not pretty. The Lord's anger is palpable and his rebuke is terrible. His words, though few, strike like rods (Rev. 2:27). Have we finally encountered a Jesus unlike the One in the Gospels? Not at all. The words Jesus spoke to the scribes and Pharisees in Matthew 23:15 could readily be applied here: "Woe to you, Jezebel, you seducer, because you prowl the churches to make one proselyte; and when you succeed, you make him twice as much a child of hell as yourself."

Does Jesus hate Jezebel? No, but he hates what she's doing.

Jesus hated Jezebel's deeds as surely as he hated the deeds of the Nicolaitans, but again, it's important to ask why. It wasn't because she was breaking the rules or compromising his standards. He hated her deeds because she was sabotaging his efforts to save the lost. By promoting sexual immorality, she was making it difficult for people to receive and respond to the authentic love of our Father.

There is a sense in which sexual sins are different from all others. In sexual sin we violate the sacredness of our own bodies, these bodies that were made for God-given and God-modeled love, for "becoming one" with another. (1 Corinthians 6:18, MSG)

86

Is it any coincidence that of all the churches in Asia, Jezebel the seductress had infiltrated the one known for walking in the *agape* love of God? Through this church, a loving God was revealing his heart to the lost and hurting people of Thyatira. The good news was bearing fruit; the church was growing in grace; lives were being transformed. Then along came Jezebel with her corrosive infidelities. What God joined together, she tore apart. What Jesus built, she undermined. A good God inspires trust, but a broken heart is distrustful, and this was the fruit of Jezebel's ministry. By encouraging immorality and adultery, she carved deep wounds in the souls of those Jesus was trying to reach.

Jezebel was a one-woman wrecking ball. She was like the deranged passenger in the lifeboat kicking holes in the floor. She had to be stopped.

If you think this is a little over the top, consider this: Thyatira was the least important of the seven cities, yet it received the longest letter and the strongest rebuke. Clearly, this was a serious concern in the eyes of the Lord.

Revelation 2:22b ...and those who commit adultery with her into great tribulation, unless they repent of her deeds.

Who committed adultery with Jezebel? Some Thyatiran Christians. Jesus said, "She seduces my servants" (Rev. 2:20). The servant of the devil was seducing the servants of the Lord.

Is Jesus going to punish these sexually immoral Christians? No. In Christ you are eternally unpunishable (see Is. 53:5). But sin still has destructive consequences. Jesus is not hard on sinners, but sin is. Sin is its own punishment.

Some translations say Jezebel's followers will suffer intensely. The picture that comes to mind is the painful suffering of sexually transmitted diseases. Those who participated in temple prostitution were risking much, especially in a world without antibiotics. Jezebel's wicked influence would reap a terrible harvest.

Is this the great tribulation that Jesus spoke of in Matthew 24:21? No, the tribulation or trouble coming to Jezebel's followers has nothing to do with the tribulation that Jesus said would come to Jerusalem.

Box 4.1: Three kinds of tribulation

Tribulation is a fact of life, but there are three kinds of tribulation. There's the tribulation that comes from the pressure of life — the pressure of work, parenting, and so forth (John 16:33). Then there's the tribulation that comes from being persecuted for your faith in Christ. This was the sort of tribulation experienced by John on Patmos (Rev. 1:9) and the saints in Smyrna (Rev. 2:9). Finally, there's the self-inflicted tribulation that comes from running after sin. It's this third kind of tribulation that Jezebel and her followers would experience (Rev. 2:22).

There are different kinds of tribulation (see Box 4.1), and sometimes tribulation can be great or extreme. In the Olivet Discourse, Jesus gave numerous signposts in connection with an unprecedented tribulation that he said was coming to Judea (see Matt. 24:15–21). Here in the seven letters, he is talking about great trouble that will come to a small group of Thyatirans if they fail to repent.

Will the sinning saints lose their salvation? No. Sin exacts a high cost, but your mistakes will never cost you your salvation. God's best is better than your worst, and his grace is greater than your sin. There are more than 130 New Testament scriptures guaranteeing the eternal security of the believer, and Jesus contradicts none of them here.[11]

Is there still time to repent? Jezebel has ignored the warnings and hardened her heart, but those who have fallen under her spell may still turn back to God.

The traditional take on this passage is that Jesus is condemning Christians, but he's not. He's dispensing grace and he does this three ways.

First, notice how Jesus addresses these sinning Christians. He does not call them fools or backsliders but "my servants" (Rev. 2:20). They are not servants of the bronzesmiths' guild or the stonemasons' lodge. They are servants of Christ. He deals with their bad behavior by reminding them of their true identity. What you do, follows who you are. If you see yourself as a servant of the Lord, you will act different from someone who sees themselves as a servant of Apollo.

Second, Jesus does not threaten the wayward saints with damnation or hell. Instead he warns them of the dangers they face (tribulation) before urging them to turn around (repent).

Third, he does not accuse them or blame them for their sin. He says they need to repent of *her* deeds. Although we are all responsible for our actions, the blame for their misdeeds lies squarely on the shoulders of the deceiver.

Like Balaam who set a trap for the children of Israel, Jezebel had enticed the saints. The harm originated with her. But all was not lost. Those who repented would be restored.

Revelation 2:23a And I will kill her children with pestilence...

Is Jesus going to kill Jezebel's kids? He's saying Jezebel has no future.

Believe it or not, but some use this verse to preach perverse lessons on church discipline, as though God could train us by killing us. Apparently the Lord needs to slaughter a few renegade Christians from time to time to keep the rest of us in line. God help us. Bad teaching thrives in the absence of good teaching, so what is Jesus really saying?

To figure out what Jesus *is* saying, it will help if we rule out what he is *not* saying. Jesus is not referring to Christians because it's her children who die, rather than the children of God. Nor is Jesus referring to Jezebel's biological children. In the old covenant there was a law that forbade putting children to death for the sins of their parents (Deu. 24:16). Since Jesus is neither a lawbreaker nor killer, Jezebel's children, if she has any, are safe.

So who are these kids who are going to be killed? History illuminates the story.

When the prophet Elijah told Jezebel's husband that the Lord would "utterly sweep you away" (1 Kings 21:21), he meant Jezebel and Ahab would leave no lineage. This prophecy was fulfilled when Jezebel's two sons and daughter were slain. Ahab had 70 other sons and they were killed as well (2 Kings 10:1–7). Death reigned in Jezebel's family. When Jesus says he's going to kill Jezebel's offspring, he's drawing a line to the Jezebel of old. He's saying her evil influence will end with her.

Since Jezebel promoted self-trust, her ministry was a cursed and barren tree. Hers was a faithless message that ultimately brought no lasting change. It was nothing like the fruit-bearing gospel of Jesus.

Kill them with *pestilence*? The original word is death, and most Bibles translate it either as "I will kill her children with death" or "I will strike her children dead." The point is that Jesus is going to ensure Jezebel leaves no legacy. This is good news for the people of Thyatira. Jezebel has done some damage; Jesus will deal with it; and there will be no lingering effects. Jezebel is going down, but the church will recover.

> **Revelation 2:23b And all the churches will know that I am he who searches the minds and hearts...**

All the churches? Everyone is going to hear about this.

Jesus intended his seven letters to enter the public domain, and they did. Two-thousand years later, the churches are still talking about them. Jezebel's bad news message is ancient history, but the good news of God's grace is bearing more fruit than ever before.

What does it mean to say Jesus searches the minds and hearts? Jesus is quoting a true prophet (see Jer. 17:10) to expose a false one. Deceivers like Jezebel may pull the wool over our eyes, but the fiery eyes of the Son of God penetrate all deception.

All the churches will know... what? They will know that Jesus is the Truth by which all imposters and deceivers shall be exposed. False prophets and false teachers may impress us with their clever words and so-called fruit, but the Lord sees their hearts. He knows who belongs to him and he knows who is pretending.

Notice that Jesus does not say, "All the churches will know that I am the one who punishes sinners with sickness and slays unrepentant believers." Yet this is the message that some take from this letter. "Jesus kills sexually immoral Christians so that the church might learn purity." It would be funny if it wasn't so sad. If Jesus killed every sinning saint, there wouldn't be any saints. The truth is *sin* kills, but Jesus saves. Sin enslaves, but Jesus sets us free. Sin makes life miserable, but Jesus empowers us to sin no more.

Revelation 2:23c ...I will give to each one of you according to your deeds.

How are we repaid for our deeds? We are judged by our response to Jesus.

In the hands of a works preacher this verse is a rod for driving the sheep. "You'd better work hard for the Lord or he'll be displeased when he comes." And the result is dead works and exhausted Christians. This is not what Jesus is talking about.

> For the Son of Man is going to come in the glory of his Father with his angels, and will then repay every man according to his deeds. (Matthew 16:27)

Jesus is not interested in dead works of the flesh, so what is the deed that is repaid? The one deed that counts is following Jesus to the cross (see Matt. 16:23). It's being baptized into his death so that we might live by his Spirit. It is trusting Jesus instead of ourselves.

> Then they asked him, "What must we do to do the works God requires?" Jesus answered, "The work of God is this: to believe in the one he has sent." (John 6:28–29, NIV)

What is the work of God? For 2,000 years people have debated this question, yet Jesus provides a straightforward answer. "Believe in him whom he has sent." Believing in Jesus is the work that is repaid when he comes.

> And I saw the dead, the great and the small, standing before the throne, and books were opened; and another book was opened, which is the Book of Life; and the dead were judged from the things which were written in the books, *according to their deeds*... and they were judged, every one of them *according to their deeds*. (Revelation 20:12–13, italics added)

The books by which the dead are judged are the records of men's thoughts and deeds (see Rom. 2:16). These books reveal that all have fallen short of God's glory.

They are the books of death. But thank God there is another book, a Book of Life. Jesus will have more to say about this book in his letter to Sardis (see Rev. 3:5).

Revelation 2:24a But I say to you, the rest who are in Thyatira, who do not hold this teaching, who have not known the deep things of Satan, as they call them…

What are the deep things of Satan? Poo nuggets passed off as pearls.

Scholars debate whether "Satan's deep secrets" is a reference to esoteric mysteries that only initiates can grasp or the Gnostic practice of exploring the depths of sin. Either way, the deep things of Satan can be contrasted with the deep things of God that are revealed to us by his Spirit (1 Cor. 2:10). The latter produces life and godliness; the former leads to sin and death.

Why did some believers fall for Jezebel's teaching? Jezebel's bad fruit—adultery and idol worship—expose her as false, yet somehow she managed to deceive Christians. How did she do this? "By her teaching," said Jesus. She seduced the saints with words.

Jezebel was articulate and compelling. She could quote scripture, and much of what she said seemed to make sense. Yet if you were paying attention, you would note that Jezebel hardly ever mentioned Jesus. The focus was always on her: "My faith, my journey, my understanding." Self-discovery was important to Jezebel. She'd invite listeners to demonstrate their maturity by moving beyond the words of Jesus and the apostles. She'd make shocking pronouncements and belittle those who disagreed with her. She would say, "I used to think the way you did but I've grown."

Listen to Jezebel and your mind might be tickled but your faith would be hammered. Her words, though eloquent, left a bad taste. Like an ill-tuned song they didn't resonate with your spirit. You'd find yourself wondering, "Did God really say that?"

Jezebel fooled some within the church, but she couldn't fool Jesus. The Lord with burning eyes saw through her empty words to the hidden message of death and destruction. He exposed her sham ministry to save his church.

Who are "the rest" in Thyatira? The saints who didn't listen to Jezebel.

As at Pergamum, there were two distinct groups in the church: those who had bought into bad teaching and those who hadn't. Jesus has a different take-away for each group. Those who followed Jezebel into immorality and idolatry need to repent. But what about the "the rest" who tolerated Jezebel? What does Jesus want them to do? He's about to tell them.

Revelation 2:24b ...I place no other burden on you.

What burdens does Jesus place on us? Only himself.

The image of Jesus burdening us seems at odds with his promise of a light and easy yoke (Matt. 11:30). But look carefully at what Jesus asks the Thyatirans to do in regards to Jezebel's deception and you will find... nothing. Which is astonishing given the mess she's made.

The letter to Thyatira is sometimes held up as a dissertation on church discipline. This is ironic given the total lack of instruction the Lord provides for fixing their problem. The saints are not told to deliver the woman to Satan for the destruction of her flesh. Nor are they told to shame or shun those who followed her. Jesus is not happy about the Jezebel situation, but everything that needs to be done, he himself will do. "I will throw... I will kill..." What is there for the Thyatirans to do but watch as Jesus delivers them from the burden of Jezebel?

The Thyatiran church made a mistake in letting this woman teach, and Christ's response is, "I got this." What a stunning picture of Jesus our Deliverer. He does not condemn the saints or threaten them with punishment. He simply promises to fix their mistake.

What a contrast with Adam, the first man. First Adam failed to keep his garden and, as a result, a serpent got in, deceived his wife, and everybody died. What did Adam do? He ran away from the problem then blamed God and Eve for everything that happened. Jesus does a far better job protecting his bride. When a serpent came into the Thyatiran garden he did not blame the church for being inattentive. He simply strapped on his bronze snake-stomping boots and dealt with the problem.

I imagine when Jesus' letter was read out in Thyatira, many breathed a sigh of relief. They knew Jezebel was trouble, but they didn't know what to do with

93

her. She was divisive and had been warned, but the church couldn't handle her. It was a horrible situation. Then came good news from Jesus. "Don't worry. I got this. You don't have to do anything about Jezebel. There's only one thing I want you to do…"

Revelation 2:25 Nevertheless what you have, hold fast until I come.

Hold fast to what? Jesus alone. In Christ we have everything we need — love, forgiveness, acceptance, holiness, righteousness. In him we have every blessing, every promise, and everything we need for newness of life. We have the mind of Christ, the Spirit of Christ, the faith of Christ. In Christ, we have it all. "Hold onto that," says Jesus. "Hold onto me."

The Thyatirans have an undeserved reputation as one of the bad churches of Revelation. "They lacked morals and doctrinal purity," said virtually every commentator I read. Yet Jesus says nothing about their lack. Instead, he reminds them of what they possess. "You already have everything they need. Hold on to it."

Those who say the Thyatirans were broken offer long lists of things they could do to fix themselves. Yet Jesus asked the saints to do one thing and only one thing: "Hold fast to me." It is the only imperative in this letter.

Christians drift off course when they lose sight of who they are and what they have. Some, like the Galatians, drift into legalism. Others, like the Thyatirans, drift into licentiousness. The remedy in either case is to lay hold of what we have in Christ Jesus. Good preachers, like Jesus and the New Testament writers, are often reminding the saints of what they already have.

Imagine getting a letter from Jesus that said, "You guys are doing great. Keep doing that. There is one problem in your group, but I'll take care of it. Just keep doing what you're doing."

That's basically what Jesus said to the Thyatirans.

Revelation 2:26 He who overcomes, and he who keeps my deeds until the end, to him I will give authority over the nations.

Who overcomes? *See Revelation 2:7b on page 34.*

What word appears more often in this letter than the others? Deeds. Jesus began this letter by commending the saints for their deeds before briefly discussing Jezebel's deeds. *Her* deeds (meaning dead works and sin), will reap destructive consequences. In contrast, *their* deeds (meaning the faith works of the saints), will be rewarded. Here at the close of his letter, Jesus encourages the saints to keep *his* deeds to the end.

What does it mean to keep his deeds? To keep his deeds is to trust and keep trusting in his work rather than your own.

Keeping his deeds is analogous to keeping his word and holding fast to his name (Rev. 2:13, 25, 3:11). It's the Revelation equivalent of continuing in the grace of God (Acts 13:43) or continuing in the faith (Col. 1:23). The meaning is the same in each case: To continue in the grace of God is to continue in Jesus. It is refusing to be suckered into sin or seduced into self-trust. It is being grounded and settled in Christ and remaining unmoved from the hope of the gospel.

In this letter Jesus mentions *his* deeds (the finished work of the cross), *your* deeds (the works of the saints), and *her* deeds (Jezebel's wicked ways). Three kinds of deeds. If our deeds are keeping his deeds, then her deeds will not distract us. But if our deeds are disconnected from his deeds, then her deeds may tempt us.

What if I don't keep his deeds to the end? Start striving in the flesh like a Galatian and you'll lose your liberty. Fall from grace like an Ephesian and you'll lose sight of your Father's love. Fool around with sin like a Thyatiran and you could suffer greatly. But you won't lose your salvation. There are always consequences to straying, but you will never cause your Father to unchild you.[12]

What does it mean to have authority over nations? Remain in the secure place of God's grace and you will reign in life (Rom. 5:17).

Authority over nations is not a distant reward offered to hard-working, high-performing Christians; it is the believer's present privilege in Christ Jesus. "All authority has been given to me in heaven and on earth" (Matt. 28:18). Jesus is the Lord of all who sits at the right hand of God. And where are we? We are not groveling at his feet like servants; we are seated with him in heavenly places (Eph.

2:6). You were a slave but Jesus has made you a king (Rev. 1:6). You have a God-given mandate to rule and reign here and now.[13]

Revelation 2:27 And he shall rule them with a rod of iron, as the vessels of the potter are broken to pieces, as I also have received authority from my Father;

Ruled with an iron rod? The word of the Lord was a sword in Pergamum and a rod in Thyatira—a rod to smash the stranglehold of the enemy and to shepherd the sheep. As is often the case with these images, Jesus is speaking of himself. He is the truth that divides (like a sword) and cannot be opposed (like a rod).

As the potter's vessels are broken? In other words, those who oppose the Lord don't stand a chance. We are living in a time of transition when the kingdom of the Lord and the kingdoms of this world coexist side by side. But ultimately only one kingdom shall endure forever (see Dan. 2:44, Rev. 11:15).

Authority from my Father? The pagan temples held no real power save that which they extorted from the fearful and superstitious Thyatirans. In contrast, the Son of God has real power given to him by the Maker of heaven and earth. The principalities and powers that terrorized Thyatira could not defeat the kingdom of God. The contest between light and darkness is no contest at all.

Revelation 2:28 And I will give him the morning star.

Who is the promised morning star? Jesus himself. "I am the Root and the Offspring of David, and the bright Morning Star" (Rev. 22:16).

Jesus is speaking of his physical return to earth. We already have his Spirit within us, but when he returns we will have him in person. When that day dawns and the morning star rises in our hearts, we will finally have our reward in full. No more sorrow, no more death. When Christ returns it will be the beginning of life such as we can only dream of.

Revelation 2:29 He who has an ear, let him hear what the Spirit says to the churches.

What does it mean to have an ear to hear? *See Revelation 2:7a on page 32.*

What does the Spirit say to the churches? *See Revelation 2:7a on page 32.*

What was Christ's message for the Thyatirans? "You guys are awesome. I marvel how you are walking in my love and growing in grace. You are bearing much fruit to my Father's glory. But why have you put up with this looney lady who calls herself a prophet? She is hurting people and I'm furious with her. My eyes are blazing! I've given her time to come to her senses, but since she won't repent, I'm ending her so-called ministry, effective immediately. She's made her bed and now she will lie in it. And those who have followed her into adultery need to repent, otherwise they will reap trouble. Sin has consequences! As for those of you who have not bought into her 'deep secrets,' I commend you. Hold onto me and let nothing move you. Don't even let this Jezebel situation distract you. I will deal with it. Allow my grace to bear fruit in your lives. Let my Father's love unleash your God-given dreams. You are my kings and co-heirs, and when I return, it will be a brand new day."

What is Christ's message for us? Want a life that matters? Then learn to distinguish dead works from faith works. Dead works are those done to curry favor with God. Law keeping, acts of charity, good deeds—anything can be a dead work if it promotes self-trust. Faith works, in contrast, flow from the abundance of God's love poured into our hearts. Faith works impart the grace of Jesus to a grace-starved world. While dead works are exhausting, faith works energize those who do them. In the end, faith works are the only works that count.

It's tempting to dismiss the Thyatirans as primitive for trusting in idols, but how different are we when we make unholy sacrifices in the pursuit of success and security? When we offer ourselves and our families on the altar of ambition, even noble ambitions like church planting and serving the poor, we set ourselves up for disaster. There is only one sacrifice that counts, and the Son of God made it. Jesus gave it all so that we may be free from the idol of Self.

We've been told that sin and sexual immorality displeases God, but we haven't been told why. God hates sin because of the pain it inflicts on those he loves. Sexual immorality is particularly damaging because it affects our capacity to receive authentic love. Yet God can mend our hurts.

Don't be impressed by those who sound wise but distract you from the simplicity that is in Christ (2 Cor. 11:3). False teachers boast of their so-called enlightenment. They delve into mystical writings and non-canonical books, but their digging only leads down. They claim to have discovered deeper mysteries, but the Son of God with burning eyes sees through them. "Know them by their fruit," said Jesus. If their message starves your faith, feeds your doubts, and leads you to rely on Self, it is not from the Lord.

Holding fast to Jesus is the key to kingly living. When you are persuaded that God is good and that he desires to be good to you, all pressure to perform evaporates. Reveling in your Father's love will lead you to walk in your God-given destiny. Begin each day by gazing upon the morning star that is Jesus. Make the Son your source and you will reign in life.

Be on your guard so that you are not carried away by the error of unprincipled men and fall from your own steadfastness, but grow in the grace and knowledge of our Lord and Savior Jesus Christ. To him be the glory, both now and to the day of eternity. Amen. (2 Peter 3:17–18)

5. SARDIS

To the angel of the church in Sardis write: He who has the seven Spirits of God and the seven stars, says this: "I know your deeds, that you have a name that you are alive, but you are dead. Wake up, and strengthen the things that remain, which were about to die; for I have not found your deeds completed in the sight of my God. So remember what you have received and heard; and keep it, and repent. Therefore if you do not wake up, I will come like a thief, and you will not know at what hour I will come to you. But you have a few people in Sardis who have not soiled their garments; and they will walk with me in white, for they are worthy. He who overcomes will thus be clothed in white garments; and I will not erase his name from the book of life, and I will confess his name before my Father and before his angels. He who has an ear, let him hear what the Spirit says to the churches." (Revelation 3:1-6)

To the east of Smyrna lies the Hermus River Valley, and above this valley rises the imposing Mount Tmolus. On one of the spurs of this mountain, the ancient kings of Lydia built an impregnable citadel that became the famed city of Sardis. The citadel sat atop sheer cliffs, and at its base the Pactolus River served as a moat. According to legend, King Midas of Phrygia rid himself of the curse of the golden touch by washing his hands in this stream.[1] The Midas story was a myth, but the gold was real, and the golden sands of the Pactolus made the kings of Sardis the wealthiest rulers in the world.

King Croesus was the most famous Sardian king, and he lived about 550 years before Christ. He was like the rich man in the parable—wealthy, content, and blinded by pride (Luke 12:16-21). Croesus had it all but lost it suddenly when Cyrus the Great took his city in a surprise attack in 546BC. The fall of Sardis was a pivot point in the history of Western civilization, for it brought the Persians to the Greek colonies of Ionia and eventually to the shores of Greece itself.

One of the changes made by the Persians was they populated Sardis with Jews. To counter an uprising in the western parts of his empire, Antiochus III (241-187BC) relocated 2,000 Jewish families to the regions of Lydia and Phrygia. In a letter to his father he said, "I am persuaded that they will be well-disposed guardians of our possessions."[2] Having seen how well the exiled Jews had adapted to life in Mesopotamia and Babylon, Antiochus knew that Jews would make good citizens. In this way the Jews came to Sardis, as well as to Philadelphia and Laodicea.

The Jews in Sardis thrived. They built a synagogue, and under Roman rule they enjoyed considerable freedom to practice their religion and customs.[3] This meant that whoever brought the gospel to Sardis had a ready audience in the synagogue. "The Messiah you've been waiting for has come!"

Today, Sardis is long gone, but at the time of Christ's letter it was a 1000-year old city with a rich history. As the former capital of the Iron Age kingdom of Lydia, the other Revelation cities, including mighty Ephesus, were at one time subject to it. But that was then. The civilizing influence of Hellenism combined with Roman road building meant that first-century Sardis was fast becoming a monument to a bygone age. The gold was gone and mountain fortresses were no longer needed. Sadly, much of the city had been reduced to rubble in the catastrophic Lydian Earthquake of AD17.

This quake, which Pliny the Elder called the greatest in living memory, devastated twelve cities of Asia, including Ephesus, Pergamum, and Philadelphia. But Sardis was hit hardest of all. The destruction was apocalyptic in scope with part of the mountain falling on the fortress.[4] When news of the devastation reached Rome, the emperor Tiberius was sufficiently moved to send the Sardians ten million sesterces — a huge sum — to aid in their reconstruction. Sardis did recover, but not to its former glory. The town that had once been a home to kings became a center of garment manufacturing.

First-century Sardis sat at the center of four important roads. The east-west road linked Sardis with Smyrna on the coast and inland Philadelphia, while the north-south road connected it to Thyatira and Ephesus. It was these trade-bearing roads that kept Sardis alive, at least for the time being. But there was no denying that Sardis' glory days were behind her. The once-proud city had become a living relic, a shadow of her former self.

Revelation 3:1a To the angel of the church in Sardis write: He who has the seven Spirits of God and the seven stars, says this:

Who is the angel of the church? *See Revelation 2:1a on page 20.*

What is the meaning of the name Sardis? Prince of joy.[5] Who was the joyful prince? No doubt it was the first Sardian ruler to discover he owned a river of gold.

What are the seven spirits of God? The Holy Spirit. God is certainly greater than our understanding, but the scriptures reveal only one God and one Spirit (Eph. 4:4–5). There aren't seven Gods or seven Holy Spirits. The "seven spirits of God" phrase could be a reference to the sevenfold ministry of the Holy Spirit.[6] Or it could be a reference to the *fullness* of the Holy Spirit, seven being the Biblical number for completion. Or it could be a reference to the diverse work of the Spirit in relation to the seven churches. Either way, it's the Holy Spirit.[7]

What are the seven stars? *See Revelation 2:1b on page 21.*

Why mention the seven stars again? Jesus is portrayed as holding the seven stars in his letters to Sardis and Ephesus. It's a similar introduction for similar cities. Both Sardis and Ephesus were, at different times, the center of gravity for western Anatolia. Sardis was the past; Ephesus was the future. Sardis had been the capital; Ephesus would become the capital. Like the Ephesians, the proud Sardians considered themselves at the center of everything. So Jesus reveals himself as in the center of the seven stars, meaning the angels or leaders of the churches, and the seven churches led by those stars.

What is the significance of this introduction? Jesus has the Holy Spirit; the Sardians do not.

The Sardians were playing church. They knew how to sound spiritual and act spiritual but they were, in fact, unspiritual. They were unacquainted with the Holy Spirit.

Revelation 3:1b I know your deeds, that you have a name that you are alive, but you are dead.

What deeds does Jesus know? *See Revelation 2:19a on page 77.*

You have a name? In contrast with the no-name church down the road in Philadelphia, the Sardian church was highly regarded. It had a reputation as a thriving fellowship. But in the Lord's eyes, that reputation was misplaced. The Sardians were all style and no substance.

Who is reputedly alive but dead? Religious unbelievers who are disconnected from the One called Life (see John 14:6).

The Sardians had a religious reputation, but they remained dead in their trespasses and sins (see Eph. 2:1). They impressed some with their religious activity, and they had an appearance of church life. But Jesus wasn't fooled. "You are dead."

Some say the Sardians were apathetic believers whose faith was waning. "They were a dying church." But the Sardians were dead, not dying. The word Jesus used to describe them literally means corpse. A corpse is not an apathetic or lazy person; a corpse is dead.

There were a few believers in this church, and Jesus will get to them in a few verses. But most of the Sardians were spiritually dead. They had not received the Spirit that gives life (Rom. 8:11). That's the bad news. The good news is that Jesus raises the dead.

Revelation 3:2a Wake up, and strengthen the things that remain, which were about to die...

What does it mean to wake up? Repent. "Wake from your sleep and turn to God."

Jesus was not speaking to lethargic Christians who need to perk up for the Lord. He's speaking to those who need to "awake and arise from the dead" (Eph. 5:14).

Like the prodigal son who "was dead and came to life again," the Sardians need rouse themselves, come to their senses, and come home to the Father (Luke 15:24).

What does it mean to strengthen that which remains? Repent before it's too late. The word for strengthen means to turn resolutely.[8] It means, get up! Move! Turn about! It is a call to immediate and definite action. It's as though the Sardians are sleeping on the train tracks and Jesus is shouting, "Wake up before it's too late!"

Who is about to die? The Sardians. The gospel isn't going to die, for the word of God never passes away. But the Sardians will pass away if they don't wake up. They are already spiritually dead; soon they will be physically dead. They may not die this year or next year, but eventually their time will run out. "The world passes away but the one who does the will of God lives forever" (1 John 2:17).

> **Revelation 3:2b ...for I have not found your deeds completed in the sight of my God.**

How were their deeds incomplete? They had not put their faith in Jesus.

Those who push dead works use this verse to burden Christians with unholy demands for religious activity. They say things like, "You have to perform for Jesus lest he find your deeds incomplete. You need to do more, study more, and pray more to maintain your fellowship with the Holy Spirit." But that's taking the Lord's words out of context. Jesus is talking to dead sinners, not living believers. It is the self-righteous—those trying to make a name for themselves—whose deeds are incomplete.

By all accounts the Sardians were plenty busy. They had acquired a reputation for their good deeds. But those who are trying to earn God's favor can never succeed. They may be slaving for the Lord, but their best will never be enough. Their deeds will always be incomplete.

In the first verse of his letter, Jesus draws attention to the Sardians' deficiency—they lacked the Holy Spirit. The fellowship of the Spirit is not something we earn through good works. The indwelling Holy Spirit is the gift of God given to all who ask (Luke 11:13).

The self-righteous Sardians had done many things *for* God, but they had not asked for anything *from* God. They were more interested in what they could give to the Lord, than what he could give to them.

Does God love these dead Sardians? Sure. But they don't know his love. There's no relationship, no intimacy, and consequently no life.

Revelation 3:3a So remember what you have received and heard; and keep it, and repent...

What had they received and heard? The gospel of Jesus Christ.

Since Sardis had a substantial Jewish population, we can assume that the gospel came to this town via the synagogue. The Sardian Jews heard the good news first, and some of them repented (see Rev. 3:4). But many did not. Hence the Lord exhorts them to "remember what you heard (the gospel) and repent (change your unbelieving minds)."

How do we keep it? To keep or hold fast to the gospel is to believe or heed it.

The gospel reveals the free gift of God's righteousness — "a righteousness that is by faith from first to last" (Rom. 1:17). One sign that a person hasn't received the gospel is they haven't received the righteousness that comes from God. They are still trying to establish their own. This is what was happening in Sardis. The Jews had heard about Jesus, but they had not grasped what Christ had done. They were boasting in their reputation when they could have been boasting in the Lord.

How do we repent? *See Revelation 2:5a on page 28.*

Wait, did this church have *unbelievers* in it? Most churches do, at least the ones making an impact in their communities.

The recording artist Keith Green once said that going to church doesn't make you a Christian any more than going to McDonald's makes you a hamburger.[9] Yet many imagine that the Revelation church communities were populated exclusively by Christians and that Christ's words for the people in those communities should be embraced by all who follow him. This is a dangerous belief indeed, and it is a key reason why much of the meaning in Jesus' letters has been lost. When you read something meant for someone else, you'll get the wrong message.

The letters to the seven churches contain words for all sorts of people, from salt-of-the-earth saints to wolves in sheep's clothing. Fail to distinguish messages meant for others from messages meant for you, and you will end up confused. You'll come away thinking that Jesus is double-minded. One minute he's full of praise; the next he's dark with rebukes. He says to hold fast; then he says to let go. He exhorts us to stand firm but he wants us to turn back. He wants us to freely receive, but he wants us to pay.

Jesus is not double-minded, but you might be if you fail to ask this question: To whom was Jesus speaking? In several of the churches Jesus distinguishes different groups of people. In Sardis, there were those who had soiled their garments and those who hadn't (see Rev. 3:4). In Pergamum there were some who held to the teaching of Balaam and some who didn't. In Thyatira there were a few who followed Jezebel into adultery and others who wanted nothing to do with her.

We shouldn't be surprised by this. Healthy, growing churches attract all sorts of people, just as Jesus did. Look at the crowds who followed him and you will find sinners and seekers, good people and bad. The Jesus of the Gospels drew the unrighteous and self-righteous, and he had different words for each. It's the same here in Revelation.

Many Christians read the letters to the seven churches and come away feeling condemned by the hard words of rebuke. These letters make them ill because they are consuming someone else's medicine. This suffering is borne of confusion. Are you a follower of Balaam? Is your name Jezebel? Are you numbered among the self-righteous who have heard the gospel and rejected it? No? Then hard words meant for them are not meant for you.

Revelation 3:3b Therefore if you do not wake up, I will come like a thief, and you will not know at what hour I will come to you.

What does it mean to wake up? *See Revelation 3:2a on page 102.*

Come like a thief? What is Jesus referring to? The day of the Lord, when he shall return unexpectedly, like a thief in the night (1 Th. 5:2).

There is some fascinating context that illuminates Christ's words. The original citadel of Sardis was situated atop a steep plateau. When Cyrus of Persia besieged their fortress, the Sardians did not bother to watch the cliffs. No one could climb the escarpment, they thought. However, Persian troops led by a soldier called Hyroiades clambered up in the dark, opened the gate, and took the city. Thus ended the reign of King Croesus.

The Citadel of Sardis, now in ruins

Like the rich man in the parable, King Croesus did not know the hour of his demise. He went to bed thinking himself safe and secure, but when he awoke all was lost. Cyrus had entered the city, like a thief in the night, and taken everything.

Amazingly, the Sardians did not learn from their mistake, for they repeated it 300 years later. With the armies of Antiochus the Great waiting outside, a nimble soldier by the name of Lagoras scaled the cliff and Sardis fell again.

To lose your city once for not paying attention is bad enough, but to lose it twice is really something. Sardis was infamous for not watching. So when Jesus says, "You guys need to wake up and watch lest I come like a thief," he is speaking their language.

What hour is Jesus coming? Not in AD70, 1000, 1984, 1988, 1999, 2012, 2017, or any hour or year that has so far been claimed. No one knows what hour the Son is coming, not even him (Matt. 24:36).[10]

"Look, I come like a thief. Blessed is the one who stays awake" (Rev. 16:15). When the Lord returns, he will arrive suddenly. People won't expect it.

How then should we live? Those slumbering in the stupor of sin need to wake up. We all need to be ready for the Master's return (Mark 13:33–37).

106

Revelation 3:4 But you have a few people in Sardis who have not soiled their garments; and they will walk with me in white, for they are worthy.

Who have not soiled their garments? Those clothed with Christ and his righteousness.

Once again, we find two groups of people within the same church: the many and the few, the soiled and the unsoiled. The many were those who were confident of their righteousness, while the few were those who had submitted to the Lord's righteousness. The many were soiled by the stain of their self-righteousness (Is. 64:6), while the few were clean because they washed their robes and made them white in the blood of the Lamb (Rev. 7:14).

Contrary to what some have taught, this has nothing to do with moral purity. Indeed, the many who were soiled were probably just as moral as the few who weren't. They were good folk who did good works and had a good name. But they didn't have the Holy Spirit. Conversely, the few who were unsoiled were not necessarily more moral than the rest. The only thing that made them different was Jesus who makes all the difference. It's Jesus who makes us washed, white, and worthy.

What are the white garments? *See Revelation 3:5a on page 108.*

Who is worthy to walk with the Lord? Those clothed with Christ and his righteousness.

Perhaps you've heard that only the top performers get to walk with the Lord. "Walking with the Lord is a reward for the faithful and spiritually pure." It's as if the kingdom of God was a multi-level marketing empire where triple-diamond achievers get exclusive access to the founder's circle. It's not true. Every believer, from the youngest to the oldest, is clothed with the robes of Christ's righteousness, and every believer walks with the Lord.

What makes us worthy in the first place? Jesus does. You may not feel worthy, but Jesus gave his life for you, so obviously you are. In his eyes, you were worth dying for. You are the pearl of great price. You might say we are all worthy, for Jesus died for all of us. But those who dismiss Christ count themselves unworthy

---

Box 5.1: The few in the new

Sardis provides a wonderful snapshot of the difference between the old and new covenants. At times of judgment in the Old Testament, God would rescue the few who were righteous before judging the many who were not. Think of righteous Noah and Lot being rescued with their families before the flood and the destruction of Sodom respectively. But here in the new covenant, Jesus has no intention of removing the few and smiting the unrighteous. Rather, he expects the many to become like the few, and the few to become many, so that all may be saved.

(see Acts 13:46). They will not walk with Christ because they choose not to. They are unworthy because they scorn the love that says they are.

You are not a special project, a basket case, or a write-off. You are worthy because Jesus says you are. Worthy means deserving or suitable, and what is a more suitable response to the grace of God but to receive it? Those who receive Christ's love and wear his righteous robes are worthy to walk with him.

What does it mean to walk with the Lord? It's sharing life together. It's living each day out of wedded union with the Lord. The Bible has a special word to describe this and it is *koinonia*. Often translated as fellowship, *koinonia* literally means participating in the abundant and joyful life of God that is in Christ Jesus (see 1 John 1:3).

In Sardis there were two kinds of people: the living and the dead. Only the living can walk with the Lord because only the living walk. To walk with the Lord is to live in intimate fellowship with Jesus. It's walking each day by faith in the new way of the Spirit.

Revelation 3:5a He who overcomes will thus be clothed in white garments, and I will not erase his name from the Book of Life...

Who overcomes? *See Revelation 2:7b on page 34.*

What are the white garments? The unsoiled garments of Christ's spotless right-eousness. As we have seen, the one who overcomes is the one who believes that Jesus is the Son of God. To believe in Christ is to be clothed in the garments of his salvation and righteousness:

> I will rejoice greatly in the Lord, my soul will exult in my God; for he has clothed me with garments of salvation, he has wrapped me with a robe of righteousness. (Isaiah 61:10a)

The white garments represent Christ's righteousness, but elsewhere in scripture they represent the righteous acts of the saints (Rev. 19:8). Which is it? Do the white garments symbolize his righteousness or our deeds? It's both. The acts of the saints are righteous because the saints are righteous, and the saints are righteous because Jesus makes them so (Rom. 5:17).[11]

The white garments also prefigure the dazzling white garments of glory that will clothe the saints when Jesus returns. When we are clothed with immortality we shall shine like the sun in the kingdom of our Father (Matt. 13:43).

What is the Book of Life? It's a heavenly register of those who inherit eternal life.

The Book of Life appears frequently in the Bible. It is mentioned by Jesus (here in the letter to Sardis and in Luke 10:20), Moses (Ex. 32:32), David (Ps. 69:28), Paul (Php. 4:3, Heb. 12:23) and several times by John (Rev. 13:8; 17:8; 20:12, 15; 21:27). The book is also hinted at by the prophets Isaiah (Is. 4:3), Daniel (Dan. 12:1), and Ezekiel (Ezek. 13:9). What is the Book of Life? It is a register of the citizens of the kingdom of God.

Isn't Jesus making a threat? No. This verse is a wonderful promise for the believer, yet in the minds of the insecure, his comforting words can be twisted into a threat. "If I don't overcome to the end, Jesus may blot me out." Relax. Jesus says it won't happen. "I will not erase your name." Since the word not in the original Greek is emphasized, we can read it as, "I will not ever, ever, under any circumstance, erase your name from the Book of Life." It is an emphatic promise. It's good news, not bad news.

Even so, some have trouble believing it. They doubt what the Lord said to the Sardians because of what he said to Moses: "Whoever has sinned against me, I will blot him out of my book" (Ex. 32:33). That is bad news indeed, for all of us have sinned and fallen short (Rom. 3:23, 5:12). None of us deserves to be in his book. Since we are all disqualified by sin, we are all in need of his grace.

> I, even I, am he who blots out your transgressions, for my own sake, and re-members your sins no more. (Isaiah 43:25, NIV)

Here is the difference between the old and new covenant: Under Moses, no one was good enough for the Book of Life; under Jesus, no believer can be blotted out. Do you see? Christ's promise to the Sardians, and by extension to all the churches, is good news, not bad. While those who lived under the old law covenant were perpetually worried that God would blot out their names from the Book of Life, this is not a worry the Christian needs to share. Under the new covenant of grace, your future is as secure as God's rock-solid promises.

The giving and recording of names is an activity that appears more than once in the seven letters. Those who receive a new name from the Lord (Pergamum), and have his name written on them (Philadelphia), and have endured for his name's sake (Ephesus), can be sure that their names will be recorded in his book and acknowledged before the Father (Sardis).

Did this promise have special relevance to Sardis? Many of the Sardian Christians were originally Jews who had been members of the synagogue. Why did they leave? Perhaps they had been expelled after refusing to utter the Curse of the Minim (see Box 5.2). Or maybe the synagogue rulers had threatened the Jewish converts with eternal damnation. "Turn your back on our law and God will blot you out of his book." To a Jewish Christian raised on the old covenant, this would have been a frightening prospect. They knew what the Lord had said to Moses. They understood that God could blot out names in the same way that city officials could deregister citizens.[12]

Jesus wanted to correct that misperception. "Fear not. I'm not a pagan official, and the citizens of my kingdom are never expelled."

Box 5.2: The Curse of the Minim

Ever since the time of Christ, Jewish believers faced expulsion from the synagogue (John 9:22, 12:42). Towards the end of the first century, a test was introduced for the purpose of outing believers. It was called the Curse of the Minim and it was incorporated into the Eighteen Benedictions of Jewish liturgy. "Let the *noẓerim* (i.e., Nazarene) and the *minim* (i.e., heretic) be destroyed in a moment. And let them be blotted out of the Book of Life and not be inscribed together with the righteous." Since anyone who followed Jesus the Nazarene would not curse themselves with these words, their silence during the benediction would expose them as Christians.[13]

Revelation 3:5b ...and I will confess his name before my Father and before his angels.

What does it mean to have Jesus confess your name? The proud Sardians were face-conscious. They were concerned about their name and reputation. Jesus exposed the futility (and fatality) of their pride before offering them a better deal. "You want a name that is known on the earth? I'll declare your name in the heavens!" Any name the Sardians had made for themselves would soon be forgotten, but their name in Jesus' book would last forever. Their name had been hailed by men, but their new name would be proclaimed by the Lord himself.

"I will confess your name before my Father." If this promise sounds familiar, it is because the Jesus of Revelation is, once again, revealing himself as the Jesus of the Gospels:

> Therefore everyone who confesses me before men, I will also confess him before my Father who is in heaven. (Matthew 10:32)

What Jesus promised the Sardians is true for every believer. "I will confess your name." But what does this mean? It may be that on Judgment Day your accusers will say, "This one is not worthy. They have done terrible things. If you are a just

God you must deny them entry!" That's bad news because the truth is you *have* done terrible things. There were times in your life when you prided yourself like a Sardian, wandered like an Ephesian, and got seduced like a Thyatiran. Your accusers have a solid case against you. But the good news is that Jesus, your friend and advocate, will stand before the Father and say, "I have redeemed this one from all claims against them. I have purchased them with my blood. This one is mine." Based on the testimony of the One called Truth, the Judge will swing the gavel and declare his righteous verdict: "Case dismissed!"

Revelation 3:6 He who has an ear, let him hear what the Spirit says to the churches.

What does it mean to have an ear to hear? *See Revelation 2:7a on page 32.*

What does the Spirit say to the churches? *See Revelation 2:7a on page 32.*

What was Christ's message for the Sardians? "You guys need to wake up and pay attention. You are playing church but you're not even saved. You've made a name for yourselves with all your religious activity, but you haven't done the one thing that matters. You have not put your faith in me. Turn to me before it's too late. Remember the gospel that you've heard and repent. You are spiritually dead, but I will give you my Spirit and add you to my Book of Life. Those who believe in me will walk with me, and I will confess their names before my heavenly Father and his angels. I also want to encourage those among you who have turned to me and are clothed with my righteousness. Fear not, for I will never erase your names from my book. Don't heed anyone who portrays me as fickle or who pressures you to prove yourself. You are worthy because I love you; you are clean because my blood has washed you; and you are saved because my Spirit dwells in you."

What is Christ's message for us? The letter to the Sardians has two takeaways. Here's the first: If you are confident of your own righteousness and take pride in your performance, Jesus wants you to know that your best will never be good enough. Your deeds, no matter how many you do, will always be incomplete.

Discard your self-righteous rags and turn to God without delay. Don't just hear the good news of his righteousness; receive it by faith.

And here's the second: If you have allowed the Lord to clothe you with the spotless raiment of his righteousness, then rejoice, for your future is secure. Although you may be kicked out of clubs, companies, and churches, the Lord will never kick you out of his kingdom. His gifts are without revocation and his Spirit within is your guarantee. Follow Jesus and your reputation may suffer, but you will be known in heaven. The Lord himself will present you to his Father and the angels.

> Therefore everyone who hears these words of mine and acts on them, may be compared to a wise man who built his house on the rock. And the rain fell, and the floods came, and the winds blew and slammed against that house; and yet it did not fall, for it had been founded on the rock. (Matthew 7:24–25)

6. PHILADELPHIA

And to the angel of the church in Philadelphia write: He who is holy, who is true, who has the key of David, who opens and no one will shut, and who shuts and no one opens, says this: "I know your deeds. Behold, I have put before you an open door which no one can shut, because you have a little power, and have kept my word, and have not denied my name. Behold, I will cause those of the synagogue of Satan, who say that they are Jews and are not, but lie—I will make them come and bow down at your feet, and make them know that I have loved you. Because you have kept the word of my perseverance, I also will keep you from the hour of testing, that hour which is about to come upon the whole world, to test those who dwell on the earth. I am coming quickly; hold fast what you have, so that no one will take your crown. He who overcomes, I will make him a pillar in the temple of my God, and he will not go out from it anymore; and I will write on him the name of my God, and the name of the city of my God, the new Jerusalem, which comes down out of heaven from my God, and my new name. He who has an ear, let him hear what the Spirit says to the churches." (Revelation 3:7–13)

Philadelphia was located about 30 miles east of Sardis on the imperial post road to Laodicea. It was a frontier town that stood on the border of Greek-speaking Lydia to the west and barbaric Phrygia to the east. Ramsay called Philadelphia a missionary city because one of its functions was to civilize the wild east by spreading Greek culture and language. It was evidently successful for by the first century the local Lydians had become Greek speakers who had all but forgotten their native tongue.[1]

Along with Sardis and ten other cities, Philadelphia was badly damaged in the great Lydian Earthquake of AD17. Although Sardis suffered the most from that quake, Philadelphia experienced nerve-wracking aftershocks for several years. The city was "ever subject to earthquakes," said Strabo, the first-century geographer.[2] The frequent shocks were so unsettling that many of the townsfolk quit the city for the safer country outside. Yet this shaky city outlasted many of its stronger rivals. While mighty Ephesus, beautiful Smyrna, and rich Laodicea now lie in ruins, Philadelphia endures today as the small and sunny Turkish city of Alaşehir, a city known for its sultana raisins.

Revelation 3:7a And to the angel of the church in Philadelphia write: He who is holy, who is true...

Who is the angel of the church? *See Revelation 2:1a on page 20.*

Who was the angel of the church at Philadelphia? Nobody knows for certain, but it might have been the highly regarded Demetrius of 3 John 1:12. If so, he was probably ordained by John.[3]

What is the meaning of the name Philadelphia? Brotherly love.[4] The city was named after its founder Attalus II Philadelphus (220–138BC), the king of Pergamum. Attalus was the younger brother and heir of the parchment champion Eumenes II. Attalus was given the nickname Philadelphus on account of the love and loyalty he showed to his older brother.

Who is holy and true? Jesus, who is the very definition of holiness and truth.

Jesus is not merely lord, but *the* Lord. In the same manner, he is not merely holy and true; he is *the* Holy and *the* True. In a world marred by sin and death, Jesus is Perfection personified. He is the Substance rather than the shadow, and the Authentic that outshines the counterfeit. He is the Truth by which all truth is measured.

Why does Jesus call himself holy? Because he's addressing a Jewish church.

Although there were Jewish communities in each of the seven cities, in Philadelphia, Sardis, and Laodicea, those communities were large and well-established. When the gospel came to Philadelphia, it would have been preached in the synagogue, and the earliest converts would have been Jews. So this was, in part, a Jewish church well-acquainted with the Old Testament.

In the Old Testament, God is often referred to as the Holy One of Israel and the God of truth.[5] By taking the name Holy and True, Jesus is revealing himself in a way that has special relevance to the Jews. He is saying, "I am the Holy and True revelation of the Holy and True God."

When Jesus began his earthly ministry, the Jews were not sure who he was. But some recognized that he was the promised Messiah. They said, "You are the Holy One of God" (John 6:69). Jesus is reaffirming that claim here. "I am the Holy One from God that you have been waiting for."

Revelation 3:7b ...who has the Key of David, who opens and no one will shut, and who shuts and no one opens, says this:

What is this key? The Key of David is another Old Testament reference that would have been familiar to Jewish listeners. This key, which unlocked the door of King Hezekiah's palace, was taken from a steward called Shebna and laid on the shoulder of a faithful servant named Eliakim (Is. 22:15–22). Eliakim decided who got to see the king and who didn't. "What he opens no one can shut, and what he shuts no one can open" (Is. 22:22). Similarly, Jesus has the keys to the kingdom of God, and no one can come to the Father except through him (John 14:6).

Yet Jesus is no mere gatekeeper, for the key upon the shoulder also symbolizes authority (see Is. 9:6). Jesus is the Son of David who sits on the Throne of David and bears the Key of David (Luke 1:32). All the riches and resources of heaven are at his disposal.

What is the significance of this introduction? Religious people have always tried to control access into the kingdom of heaven, but Jesus, the holder of the David's key, decides who gets to come in.

The transfer of the key from unfaithful Shebna to Eliakim mirrors Israel's fall from grace. Shebna, whose name means vigor, lost the key to Eliakim, whose name means resurrected of God. Shebna represents the religious Jews who served in the vigor of their own strength but who shut the door to the kingdom of heaven. "You yourselves do not enter," said Jesus to the scribes and Pharisees. "Nor will you let those enter who are trying to" (Matt. 23:13). In contrast, Eliakim represents the resurrected Messiah who opens doors and invites all to come in.

In Philadelphia, religious Jews from the synagogue made it difficult for people to turn to God. They hindered the gospel and opposed the Christians. Jesus wanted the church to know that he holds the key, and that no man can shut any door that he opens.

6. PHILADELPHIA

Revelation 3:8a I know your deeds. Behold, I have put before you an open door which no one can shut...

What deeds does Jesus know? *See Revelation 2:19a on page 77.*

What is the open door? It's an opportunity to preach the gospel.

When Paul went to Troas, he found that "the Lord had opened a door" for him (2 Cor. 2:12). And he lingered in Ephesus because "a great door for effective work" had opened (1 Cor. 16:9).

An open door is what you have when people respond to the gospel and come to Jesus. The Apostle Paul craved open doors and was in the habit of praying for them (Col. 4:3). If he had been alive and had heard there was an open door in Philadelphia, he would've gone there in a flash.

Who opens the door? Not us.

> When they had arrived and gathered the church together, they began to report all things that God had done with them and how *he had opened a door of faith to the Gentiles.* (Acts 14:27, italics added)

The Lord-with-a-key opens doors for his gospel, and often he does so in the most unexpected places. Philadelphia, a city of earthquakes and hostile Jews, would not have ranked high on our list of places to evangelize. Yet this town was ripe for the gospel. It was full of low-hanging fruit.

What exactly was the open door? In the long run it could have been the un-reached people of Phrygia to the east, but the immediate opportunity for the gospel was found in the large Jewish community within Philadelphia. In this letter, Jesus prophesies that some of the religious Jews who are opposing the church are going to get saved.

Revelation 3:8b ...because you have a little power, and have kept my word, and have not denied my name.

A little power? A church with little power is a small or weak church. The Philadelphians weren't anything special. They lacked the resources of their Laodicean neighbors, and they didn't have the reputation of the Sardians. Like David, the shepherd boy, they were of little account in the eyes of man. But weakness is no barrier to God. If anything, it's an advantage because God chooses the weak things of the world to shame the strong (1 Cor. 1:27).

A God who shares the stage with no one seems to delight in choosing the least qualified and the most unlikely. When he needed a man to lead Israel against the Midianites, he chose chicken-hearted Gideon. When he needed a herald for the gospel of grace, he chose law-loving Saul. And when he needed a father of many nations, he chose grey-haired Abram. In the economy of grace, the weak and unqualified seem to have the inside track.

If you were to tour the churches of Asia, you might be dazzled by the energetic Ephesians, the affluent Laodiceans, and the spiritual Sardians. And you might be tempted to dismiss the small Philadelphian church as inconsequential. But Philadelphia was where the action was. Jesus had given this little church an open door that no one could shut. What a wonderful encouragement for those of us who think we have nothing to offer. You may have no money, no reputation, no ability, no connections, no education, and no chance, but as long as you have the Lord, you have everything you need. You may have no power, but the Lord-with-the-key has given you authority over all the power of the enemy (Luke 10:19).

How had they kept his word? They believed Jesus and took him at his word.

What made the Philadelphians special was this: They were believing believers who were persuaded that the Lord is good and trustworthy. This is the only clue to their commendation. Nothing else is recorded. Search the letter to the Philadelphians and you will not find seven steps to success, or twelve strategies for church outreach. The Philadelphians simply believed Jesus, and that made all the difference.

The question to ask is not why the Philadelphians had an open door, but why some of the other churches weren't as fruitful. The answer is they were captive to unbelief. They put little stock in the grace of God. The Ephesians' unbelief was evident in the way they were working themselves to death. The Sardians' unbelief was in their refusal to receive the gospel. And the Laodiceans' unbelief was in their boast that they needed nothing from God. Unbelief takes many forms and not even believers, strangely, are immune from its insidious effects. But whenever the promises of God are dismissed or doubted, the result is barrenness. Apart from him we can do nothing.

How had they not denied his name? The Philadelphians had endured some kind of test, such as the Curse of the Minim (see previous chapter). They had been challenged to renounce the name of the Lord, perhaps under threat of expulsion from the synagogue, but they had refused to do so.

The Ephesians endured for the sake of his name (Rev. 2:3); the Pergamenes held fast to his name (Rev. 2:13); and the Philadelphians did not deny his name (Rev. 3:8). The common element in all three churches was opposition: false apostles in Ephesus, Roman hostility in Pergamum, and religious oppression in Philadelphia.

Some believe the Philadelphians suffered no trouble because Jesus promised to keep them from the hour of testing (see Rev. 3:10). But it is only in the face of opposition that we have the opportunity to deny his name. Polycarp of Smyrna was pressured to renounce the name of Jesus or be burned at the stake, and the believers at Philadelphia experienced similar pressure. In fact, when Polycarp was martyred, eleven Christians from Philadelphia were killed with him.[6]

What if they had denied his name? Jesus would still love them.

Many believers worry that they might deny Jesus under pressure. They fear that if someone held a gun to their head and forced them to renounce the name of the Lord, they'd capitulate and be damned for all time. They worry because Jesus said, "Whoever denies me before men, I will deny before my Father in heaven" (Matt. 10:33). But Jesus wasn't talking about Christians with guns to their heads; he was talking about those who refuse to confess him as Lord.

For if we died with him, we will also live with him… If we deny him, he also will deny us. If we are faithless, he remains faithful, for he cannot deny himself. (2 Timothy 2:11–13)

119

This verse is contrasting unbelievers (who deny Jesus) with believers (who identify with Christ's death). Those who refuse salvation shall not have it, but those who have died with Christ will never be cast away. Even if we falter at the last hurdle and prove faithless, he remains faithful. One with the Lord, your future is safe, for he cannot deny himself.

This anxiety that we might fail Christ under pressure and be damned reveals a fundamental insecurity, a hairline crack in our faith. We repair it by fixing our eyes on Jesus and fortifying our minds with the many promises of his word. "No one can snatch you from my strong right hand," said Jesus. "I will never let you go." What a promise! Even if we let him go, he will never let go of us. This is good news. And if you believe it, you will find the strength to hold on to him no matter what.

Revelation 3:9a Behold, I will cause those of the synagogue of Satan, who say that they are Jews and are not, but lie...

What is the synagogue of Satan? *See Revelation 2:9b on page 43.*

Who are the Jews that are not Jews? *See Revelation 2:9b on page 43.*

Who are the Jews that lie? Religious haters in the slander business.

The Jews of Philadelphia had been there for 300 years. They were an established and influential community within the city. In contrast, the church of Philadelphia was new and small. All the evidence suggests that the big and powerful synagogue was picking on the little church. Religious Jews were bullying the Christian Jews.

When Jesus refers to the synagogue of Satan, he is not talking about Jews in general, of which there were some in the church. He's talking about *religious* Jews who despised the Jewish Christians as traitors and enemies of God. These fanatics thought nothing of flogging Christians with whips (2 Cor. 11:24). In the name of their religion they would incite the Romans to harass and persecute the followers of Jesus (e.g., Acts 17:5–8).

Open doors attract opposition. In speaking of his kingdom Jesus said, "Many will try to enter and will not be able to" (Luke 13:24). The reason they can't enter is because outside the door there is a bouncer called Religion. This bouncer is a thug who speaks the devil's lies: "You can't come in here looking like that! You're a sinner and a lawbreaker. You need to get cleaned up before you can approach the Lord." This is what was happening in Philadelphia. The Christians were preaching the gospel of the kingdom, but those coming in were being hindered by the "Jews who lie." They lied about the gospel. "You need to keep the law to become acceptable to God." And they lied about those preaching it. "These heretics are sending people to hell."

It was hard going for the small church. Their enemies were organized, well-resourced, and highly motivated. They knew how to work the system. There must have been times when the saints felt like they were going to be shut down by irresistible forces. They needed encouragement, and that's what Jesus gave them. "I've given you an open door that no one can shut." What a reassuring word from the Lord-with-a-key.

Revelation 3:9b ...I will make them come and bow down at your feet, and make them know that I have loved you.

Who will come and bow? The religious Jews who had been attacking the church.

Will the religious Jews actually bow to the church? Jesus is saying the hostile Jews will come to realize that those in the church are God's people. In the city of brotherly love, Jesus will show the Jews who his real brothers are.

This is some prophecy. For hundreds of years, the Jews were mistreated by Gentile nations. They had been besieged, enslaved, mocked, and murdered. Throughout this dark time, they had been encouraged by the thought that one day vindication would come.

> The sons of those who afflicted you will come bowing to you, and all those who despised you will bow themselves at the soles of your feet (Isaiah 60:14a)

Eventually the tables would turn and the scales of justice would balance. The oppressors of the Jews would finally recognize them as God's people and pay homage. They would say, "Let us go with you, for we have heard that God is with you" (Zech. 8:23).

But Jesus upends the old prophecy by saying *the Jews* will come and bow to the church. Contrary to all expectation, they will be the ones who admit their error and declare, "God is with you." It's a startling reversal. How could this have happened? How did the Jews find themselves on the wrong side of the prophecy?

In rejecting God's Son, the Jews cut themselves off as a nation. They effectively said, "We are no longer God's people." By persecuting Jesus and those who followed him, the oppressed became the oppressor; the victims became the bullies. Promises that God had made to old Israel now applied to the new Israel, namely a church composed of Jews, Gentiles, and powerless Philadelphians.

"They will come and bow." Such a pronouncement would have stunned the religious Jews, but it would not have surprised Jewish converts familiar with another ancient prophecy:

> Afterward the sons of Israel will return and seek the Lord their God and David their king; and they will come trembling to the Lord and to his goodness in the last days. (Hosea 3:5)

The sons of Israel rebelled against David their king when they rejected his grandson Rehoboam (1 Kings 12:16). But a day would come, said Hosea, when they would return to David's heir. Hosea was referring to Jesus (see Matt. 1:1). His prophecy was fulfilled on the Day of Pentecost when 3,000 Jews heard the good news, were cut to the heart, and repented. And it was further fulfilled in Philadelphia whenever a lost son of Israel came to the Lord.

How would Jesus make the Jews know that he loved the church? He was going to love them into the kingdom.

Imagine a Philadelphian Jew named Alexander. He hates Christians, and he believes that God hates them too. "They are uncircumcised law breakers!" Alexander considers it his holy duty to oppose Christians at every turn, so he spreads lies about them. He tells his neighbors they are troublemakers and the cause of all misfortune. "The earthquakes are God's judgment for tolerating these heathens." He says they are disloyal because they refuse to say, "Caesar is Lord." (That Alexander pays money to avoid this oath is neither here nor there.) As far as Alexander is concerned, the only good Christian is a dead Christian. When Polycarp and the eleven from Philadelphia are sentenced to death, Alexander rejoices that God's work has been done. He travels to Smyrna to see the hated Christians burn. He even helps to gather wood for the fire.

But something happens to Alexander. He hears the gospel and is radically changed by the love of Jesus.

"The rumors were true. The Nazarene is the risen Son of God!"

He shares this good news with his friends and neighbors but is kicked out of the synagogue. So he comes to the church, bowing in apology.

"Forgive me. I was wrong. Now I know that God loves you and is with you."

Alexander is unsure of how the Christians will treat him. He imagines they will hate him for the damage he's done. Instead, they welcome him with open arms as one of their own. Then his new Christian brothers and sisters tell him something he never forgets as long as he lives.

"Jesus sent us a letter. He told us you were coming."

Revelation 3:10a Because you have kept the word of my perseverance...

What is the word of his perseverance? It's the good news that Jesus has persevered and overcome the world. It's the joyful revelation that because Jesus has done it all, you have nothing to prove.

To keep his word (Rev. 3:8) or keep his deeds (Rev. 2:26) or keep his faith (Rev. 2:13) or keep the word of his perseverance (Rev. 3:10) is to believe in Jesus and his finished work. It's guarding the truth, continuing in the faith, and staying settled on the rock. It is refusing to be tempted into the dead works of religion and unbelief.

How might they have failed to keep the word of his perseverance? They could have fallen under the law.

To the Jewish mind, the Christians were lawless. They claimed to follow God yet they did not practice circumcision or live by the Law of Moses (see Acts 15:5). Worst of all, they worshipped a dead rabbi as though he was the Son of God. This was unacceptable. The Christians needed to be brought into line. Such was the mindset that opposed the believers in Philadelphia.

Like the Galatians, the Philadelphians were pressured to accept another gospel, one that emphasized ritual observance of the law. But unlike the Galatians, the Philadelphians didn't listen. They remained true to Christ and refused to allow themselves to become burdened by a yoke of slavery.

How can you be sure this is about the law? Jesus never mentions the law in his letters—why would he?—but no other issue was of greater concern to religious Jews. We can be certain this was the flash-point in Philadelphia, because of another letter received by the church. This letter came from Ignatius of Antioch. Ignatius was a friend of Polycarp's, and both had been trained by the legendary John. In his letter, Ignatius urged the Philadelphians to resist all forms of law.

> If anyone preach the Jewish law unto you, listen not to him… (If any) persons do not speak concerning Jesus Christ, they are in my judgment but as monuments and sepulchers of the dead, upon which are written only the names of men.[7]

Ignatius seems to have understood that if you live under law, you fall from grace. This happens because law-keeping puts the focus on us and our performance while distracting us from Jesus and his.

What is the law? In the first century, law preaching meant preaching the Law of Moses (Acts 15:21). But in the 21st century, just about anything can be turned into a law—even the words of Jesus to the Philadelphians.

"Because you have kept the word of my perseverance, I also will keep you from the hour of testing." Some twist our Savior's beautiful words into a Christian fitness test. They say you have to persevere and endure to be saved. You have to keep Christ's commands and maintain an erect and noble bearing under pressure. Fail to persevere and you risk punishment, even damnation.

This old covenant interpretation even appears in some English Bibles. "Because you have kept my command to endure…." What command?! There is no command. Jesus is not even talking about the Philadelphians' endurance or perseverance; he's commending them for keeping the word of *his* perseverance. "Because you kept my command… I will keep you from the hour of trial." What is this? The Old Testament?! Talk about putting an old covenant spin on a new covenant promise.

Bad translations put price tags on the grace of God and turn gifts into wages; good translations reveal the good news of Jesus. We are not kept from the coming trial because we endure; we are kept because Christ has endured.

Revelation 3:10b …I also will keep you from the hour of testing, that hour which is about to come upon the whole world, to test those who dwell on the earth.

What is the hour of testing coming on the whole world? Judgment Day, a day of shaking.

To a Philadelphian, the hour of testing would evoke anxious memories of earthquakes and houses falling down. When Jesus says such an hour is coming on the whole world, they might imagine a global shaking, and they would not be far wrong.

> At that time his voice shook the earth, but now he has promised, "Once more I will shake not only the earth but also the heavens." The words "once more" indicate the removing of what can be shaken — that is, created things — so that what cannot be shaken may remain. (Hebrews 12:26–27, NIV)

Jesus was not referring to the destruction of Jerusalem, which had already happened and was a localized event. Nor was he referring to the temptations and trials of everyday life. He was referring to an hour (a finite time period) of testing (or shaking) that will affect everyone (the whole world) except the Philadelphians (and all Christians).

> Therefore, since we are receiving a kingdom that cannot be shaken, let us be thankful, and so worship God acceptably with reverence and awe. (Hebrews 12:28, NIV)

When Jesus returns, everything will be tested. Those things that are opposed to Christ will be shaken, but the believer who has been tested and approved in Christ will stand firm. Thus the hour of testing or judgment (see Rev. 14:7) is for the world, not the church. It's for those who dwell upon the earth, rather than the citizens of an unshakeable kingdom.

Revelation 3:11 I am coming quickly; hold fast what you have, so that no one will take your crown.

Is Jesus coming soon? Not soon, but quickly.

Some believe that Christ came in judgment and destroyed Jerusalem in AD70. One of the arguments used to support this teaching is Christ's repeated promise of coming soon. However, Jesus never said he was coming soon. How could he (see Matt. 24:36)? Rather, Jesus said he would come *quickly*. "When my Father gives the word, I will come swiftly and without delay."[8]

Hold fast to what? Jesus.

The Philadelphians are often considered the best of the seven churches while the Thyatirans are typically dismissed as the worst, yet Jesus asks both churches to do one thing only: hold fast to him. This is significant: whatever you are facing, whether you are facing troubles outside or in, Jesus is your answer. He is your hope, your help, and your guiding hand. *See also Revelation 2:25 on page 94.*

Can we lose our crown? Not if we are talking about the crown of life (see Revelation 2:10c). Some worry that if we don't endure and hold fast we will lose our salvation, but that can't happen. Just as we don't merit salvation through our good deeds, we don't lose it by our bad. But there is another kind of crown that can be lost and that crown is people. Paul said to the Thessalonians, "What is the crown in which we will glory in the presence of our Lord Jesus when he comes? Is it not you?" (1 Th. 2:19). The Thessalonians were Paul's crown and glory, and it's this sort of crown that Jesus is describing here.

The Bible is full of stories of people who had their crown or inheritance taken by another: Jacob took Esau's place, David took Saul's, Eliakim took Shebna's, and the Gentiles took the Jews'.[9] The danger here is that the Philadelphians will be added to this list of those who lost their crown.

The Lord had given them an open door, but they were facing stiff opposition from the synagogue of Satan. If the church was bullied into silence, people wouldn't hear the good news of Jesus, and the opportunity to win souls would slip through their fingers. Hence the Lord's encouragement: "Hold fast to what you have (keep trusting in Jesus), so that no one will take your crown (those people who are your inheritance)."

Revelation 3:12a He who overcomes, I will make him a pillar in the temple of my God, and he will not go out from it anymore...

Who overcomes? *See Revelation 2:7b on page 34.*

Why a pillar? We are weak and prone to falling, but Jesus makes us strong as pillars.

There is a perception that only influential Christians are pillars in the church, but in Christ we are all pillars. This is all to the glory of the Lord. We stand by grace; we hold fast by grace; we endure by grace. Every single one of us is a monument to the grace of God.

What is the temple of God? The body of believers, the household of faith.

The Jesus of the Gospels said he would raise a temple and build a church (Matt. 16:18, John 2:19), and here we see how he planned to do that: by turning people into pillars. Once upon a time, the presence of God inhabited a manmade temple, but now the dwelling place of the Lord is his church (Eph. 2:21–22). "Do you not know that you are the temple of God?" (1 Cor. 3:16).

What does it mean to go out no more? Peace and security. Philadelphia was infamous for its frequent quakes and aftershocks. When the buildings began to shake, the Philadelphians would run out into the open air. The tremors were so frequent that running out almost became a way of life. When the shakes ended, the Philadelphians would return to find their homes cracked and damaged.

Earthquakes and aftershocks exact a high toll on one's mental health. When Jesus says, "You will not go out any more," he's saying, "I'm bringing an end to your anxiety." It's a comforting word for stressed-out people.

Jesus does not promise to end the tremors that shake our life, but he does offer his rock-solid word to help us endure. "I will make you a pillar in the temple of my God." The faithless are restless, but those who are grounded on the Rock of Calvary have peace during times of upheaval. Their world might shake and collapse, but they stand firm on the word of the Lord.

> **Revelation 3:12b ...and I will write on him the name of my God, and the name of the city of my God, the new Jerusalem, which comes down out of heaven from my God, and my new name.**

What is the significance of these three names? Favor, family, and friendship.

"I will write on him the name of my God." In the old covenant the priests put the name of God on the children of Israel by blessing them (Num. 6:24–27). When Jesus says he will write God's name on us, he's marking us for blessing. As a child of God, you are stamped highly favored.

"I will write on him the name of the city of my God." According to the prophets, the name of the New Jerusalem was to be *Jehovah-shammah*, meaning "the Lord is there" (Ezek: 48:35). Ancient cities were named after distant emperors, but the Holy City, which is the church, is the Lord's dwelling place. He is there. He is not someplace else. This name conveys a sense of family because "Jerusalem above is our mother" (Gal. 4:26). You are a not a slave of empire, but a free child of Jerusalem, and Christ dwells in you.[10]

"I will write on him my new name." To be marked with the name of Jesus means you belong to the Lord. You bear his Spirit as a seal of his ownership and a guarantee of his precious promises.

What is the new name of Jesus? Jesus has many names and titles, and some of them are mysterious and unknown (Rev. 19:12). What new name is Jesus referring to here? The answer is in the adjective *new*. Jesus is talking about a name or title that is new to him, and that was *kyrios* or Lord or "the One who is supreme above all."

When Jesus walked the earth he was known as Jesus of Nazareth. But after he ascended to heaven he was given a new name above every name, and that name is Lord (Php. 2:9–11). On the Day of Pentecost, Peter stood up and preached the new name of the Lord:

Fellow Israelites, listen to this: Jesus of Nazareth was a man accredited by God to you by miracles, wonders, and signs... Therefore let all Israel be assured of this: God has made this Jesus, whom you crucified, both Lord and Messiah. (Acts 2:22, 36, NIV)

Peter urged his listeners to call on the name of the Lord and be saved (Acts 2:21). In Asia, the saints refused to call anyone Lord but Jesus. Like the apostles and the martyrs, they bore his new name with boldness, and Jesus commended them for it (see Rev. 3:8). Just as the old covenant priests wrote the name of God on the children of Israel by blessing them, the high priest of the new covenant writes his new name on us by demonstrating his saving power. Put it altogether and Jesus is saying this: "He who overcomes (i.e., believes in me), I will save. I will write my new name on them — that name that is above all names — and nothing and no one will ever separate them from my love." It's an emphatic declaration of friendship and salvation and aid and protection from the best Friend you could ever have.

What's with all these names? Jesus told the Pergamenes that overcomers would get a new name, but Jesus told the Philadelphians that they would get *three* new names. It's name inflation. Why did the Philadelphians get so many names? Because they loved new names. They collected them, like stamps.

After Philadelphia was leveled in the big quake of AD17, the emperor granted tax relief to the city to assist with the rebuild. In gratitude, the Philadelphians changed the name of their city to Neocaesarea, the City of the Young Caesar. Then 50 years later they changed their name again to Flavia, in honor of the family name of Emperor Vespasian. The Philadelphians changed names like people change cars. No other city did this. These new names didn't stick, but clearly this was a town where the locals liked to identify with powerful patriarchs.

So Jesus says to the Philadelphians, "You like new names? I'll give you a name to top all names. I'll give you the name of my God, which is the highest honor of all. And I'll give you the name of the city of my God because you are citizens of heaven. But wait, there's more. I will also give you my new name, which is to say I will give you myself — my life, my identity, my all."

The weak and friendless Philadelphians would have loved this. They were the smallest church in Asia, yet the Son of God was speaking to them in a language only a Philadelphian could appreciate.

Add this promise to the one made to the Sardians and we see a lovely complementarity: First, Jesus promises to never remove our names from his book, then he promises to write his name on us three different ways. In Christ, we are well-named and well-kept.

What about all these "I wills" of Jesus?

The Philadelphians are often esteemed as a model church because Jesus never rebuked them—as though escaping censure was the high point of Christian living. (What a sad way to read these love letters from Jesus. "I got a letter from the Lord and he didn't scold or threaten to kill me. I'm so blessed.") Each of the seven letters reveals something of the goodness of God, but nowhere does God's grace and kindness shine brighter than in this letter to the powerless Philadelphians. In less than 250 words, the Lord gives one of the most stunning summaries of the hope held out in the gospel, and he does this by making promises.

Because many people don't know what makes the new covenant *new*, they miss these treasures. They read these letters with an old covenant mindset and come away quaking in their boots. This is why it's essential to understand the difference between the old and new covenants.[11]

The old covenant was characterized by people making promises to God, but the new covenant of grace is based on God's unbreakable promises to us. In the old covenant people said, "We will," as in, "We will do everything the Lord says" (Ex. 19:8). But in the new covenant God says "I will." The old covenant failed because we can't keep our promises, but the new endures because God is eternally faithful.

In each letter to the seven churches, Jesus says "I will" at least one time. By making promises to us, Jesus is speaking the language of the new covenant. But to the Philadelphians Jesus says, "I will" no less than eight times: *I will* make them come and bow down at your feet (Rev. 3:9); *I will* make them know that I have loved you. (Rev. 3:9); *I will* keep you from the hour of testing (Rev. 3:10); *I will* come quickly (Rev. 3:11); *I will* make you a pillar (Rev. 3:12); *I will* write on you the name of my God (Rev. 3:12); *I will* write on you the name of the city of my God (Rev. 3:12); and *I will* write on you my new name (Rev. 3:12).

These promises are not carrots to induce proper behavior. Nor are they performance incentives offered to high achievers. They are pledges from a good God who longs to bless us and who always keeps his word. They are vows guaranteed by the perfect work of Christ (2 Cor. 1:20).

The Philadelphians were highly favored to receive eight beautiful promises. Does this mean they were more special than the rest of us? Not at all. Christ's words for them are for all the churches. So how come the other six churches never got these promises? They weren't ready. The Ephesians had wandered, the Smyrneans were in trouble, the Pergamenes and Thyatirans were conflicted, the Laodiceans were lukewarm, and the Sardians were dead. The other churches all had major problems and Jesus needed to deal with those first.

The Philadelphians were different. They were drinking grace straight from the tap. They did not get more promises because they were better or more deserving but because they were believing-believers. They took God at his word. They had those little fridge magnets that said, "God said it, I believe it, that settles it." Because they treasured the promises of God, Jesus blessed them with more. They who had been faithful with a little, found themselves with a lot.

Revelation 3:13 He who has an ear, let him hear what the Spirit says to the churches.

What does it mean to have an ear to hear? *See Revelation 2:7a on page 32.*

What does the Spirit say to the churches? *See Revelation 2:7a on page 32.*

What was Christ's message for the Philadelphians? "You guys are amazing. Everyone thinks you're this insignificant little church, but they forget that my Father chooses the weak things of the world to shame the wise. You are punching above your weight because you believe my gospel. You are bearing fruit because you are abiding in my love. You are fully persuaded that God is good. And this hostility that you're experiencing from your neighbors is a reaction to that.

They're trying to shut you down, but I'm the one holding the keys. I'm personally going to make sure you remain open for business. They're jealous, but even they will come to see that God's favor is upon you. Don't give up. You have a wonderful inheritance and it's *them*, your neighbors. They are my harvest and your crown. Don't let anything move you from the secure foundation of my love. You guys are my monuments of grace!"

What is Christ's message for us? In the economy of grace, size doesn't matter, so don't let your lack hold you back. You may be a no-name believer with no reputation, no platform, no nothing, but that is no barrier to the Maker of heaven and earth. All you need is to believe that your Father is good and that he has good things in store for you.

Perhaps you have heard that success is the result of persevering and never giving up. In this world, that may be true. But in the kingdom it is the word of *his* perseverance we're supposed to keep. Jesus has done the hard work; our part is to reap what he has sown. Jesus opens the doors; our part is to walk through them.

Evangelism done under compulsion is a drudge, but when we align ourselves with what God is doing, the results are supernatural. "I do what I see my Father doing," said Jesus, and so do we. Yet open doors attract opposition. Make a mark for God and you can expect pushback. The temptation will be to draw back, even quit. Don't let intimidation rob you of your crown. God has given you an inheritance, and it's people. Those who encounter the grace of God through you are your crown and joy. Hold fast to Jesus and no one will take your crown. Stand firm on the solid rock and you will be a pillar in times of shaking.

Rejoice in the Lord always; again I will say, rejoice! …And my God will supply all your needs according to his riches in glory in Christ Jesus. (Philippians 4:4, 19)

7. LAODICEA

To the angel of the church in Laodicea write: The Amen, the faithful and true Witness, the Beginning of the creation of God, says this: "I know your deeds, that you are neither cold nor hot; I wish that you were cold or hot. So because you are lukewarm, and neither hot nor cold, I will spit you out of my mouth. Because you say, 'I am rich, and have become wealthy, and have need of nothing,' and you do not know that you are wretched and miserable and poor and blind and naked, I advise you to buy from me gold refined by fire so that you may become rich, and white garments so that you may clothe yourself, and that the shame of your nakedness will not be revealed; and eye salve to anoint your eyes so that you may see. Those whom I love, I reprove and discipline; therefore be zealous and repent. Behold, I stand at the door and knock; if anyone hears my voice and opens the door, I will come in to him and will dine with him, and he with me. He who overcomes, I will grant to him to sit down with me on my throne, as I also overcame and sat down with my Father on his throne. He who has an ear, let him hear what the Spirit says to the churches." (Revelation 3:14–22)

Our final stop on the mail circuit brings us to the most famous city in Revelation, Laodicea. Situated in the Lycus River Valley, in the region of Phrygia, Laodicea was a little under 100 miles east of Ephesus. And it was the road to Ephesus that made Laodicea an important center of first-century trade. Goods from the east entered Laodicea through the Syrian Gate and were sent out west through the Ephesian Gate.[1]

Much of Laodicea was built around 250BC by Antiochus II (286–246 BC), the king of the Seleucid Empire. He named the town after Laodice his wife. Was she impressed? Not for long. A few years later she murdered her husband after he dumped her for a Ptolemaic princess.

The city of Laodicea passed into Roman hands at the end of the Roman-Seleucid War in 188BC. The victorious Romans gave Laodicea to the Pergamenes to thank them for their aid in the war; fifty-five years later, the Pergamenes gave it back.

Under Roman rule, the city thrived. Laodicea became a banking and financial center, a place where emperors could cash checks. It had a massive stadium, the outlines of which you can still see today.[2] It had three theatres as well as temples to an assortment of gods and goddesses. Laodicea also had a medical school that may have been associated with the manufacture of Phrygian powder. Crushed from local stone, this powder was supposed to do wonders for your eyesight.

What was the secret to Laodicea's success? In a word: wool. Like other Asian cities, Laodicea relied heavily on wool-based industries such as textile and garment manufacturing. It was a competitive business, but the Laodiceans enjoyed a unique advantage: their wool was glossy black. Strabo the geographer reported that Laodicean sheep were acclaimed for their soft, raven-black wool and "the Laodiceans derive splendid revenue from it."[3] Black tunics made in Laodicea were hot-ticket items that were exported all over the Roman world.

In the Bible, Laodicea is linked with two nearby towns: Hierapolis, seven miles to the north, and Colossae, nine miles to the east. All three cities prospered from regional trade, but Laodicea was the greatest city in the valley.

Did the Apostle Paul ever visit Laodicea? This is one of the mysteries of the Bible. It's hard to imagine Paul not going to such an important city. How could he have missed it? Plus, Laodicea was on the overland route to Ephesus. Yet there's no mention in the scriptures of Paul ever visiting Laodicea or nearby Colossae, and in his letter to the Colossians, Paul acknowledges that they had not heard the gospel from him but Epaphras (Col. 1:7).

Paul may not have gone there, but we know from his letter to the Colossians that Laodicea was on his mind. "I want you to know how hard I am contending for you and those at Laodicea" (Col. 2:1). In fact, Paul also sent a letter to the Laodiceans, and he told the Colossians that both churches should swap their letters after they had read them (Col. 4:16). It seems Paul was concerned about the Laodiceans, and it's not until we read the letter from Jesus that we find out why.

Christ's letter to the Laodiceans stands out among the seven for one startling reason: Jesus has nothing good to say about the church. Not one word. The dead church of Sardis had a faithful few, but in Laodicea no one is praiseworthy. "The Laodicean Church is the only one which is absolutely and wholly condemned," said Ramsay.[4] Since there is no condemnation to those in Christ, we might wonder whether this was a church in anything other than name.[5]

Revelation 3:14 To the angel of the church in Laodicea write: The Amen, the faithful and true Witness, the Beginning of the creation of God, says this:

Who is the angel of the church? *See Revelation 2:1a on page 20.*

What is the meaning of the name Laodicea? Laodicea was named after the murderous Seleucid Queen Laodice. Her name was made up of two Greek words: *laos*, meaning people, and *dike*, meaning justice or judgment. Hence Laodicea means the judging people or people rule.[6] It's an apt name for a church that was ruled by people. King Jesus did not rule; the people did.

Who was the angel of the church at Laodicea? Possibly Archippus, the son of Philemon (Philemon 1:2).[7]

The church in Laodicea may have been planted by some anonymous Jew from Phrygia who happened to be in Jerusalem on the Day of Pentecost (see Acts 2:10). Or perhaps Epaphras took the gospel there on his journey from Ephesus to Colossae. By the time of Paul, this church was meeting in the house of a woman called Nympha (Col. 4:15), and Archippus seems to have been in charge. We know this because Paul says to him, "Be sure to do the work the Lord gave you" (Col. 4:17). In other words, "Do your job."

Was Archippus not doing his job? Was he a bad bishop, negligent in preaching the gospel? Was he the reason this church was so strenuously rebuked by the Lord? Nobody knows, but it's an intriguing possibility.

Why does Jesus call himself the Amen? Because he is the Yes and Amen and the underwriter of all the promises of the new covenant (2 Cor. 1:20).

Why does Jesus call himself the faithful and true Witness? He is faithful and true in contrast with the Laodiceans who were faithless and false. Yet Jesus is not merely faithful and true; he is *the Amen*, faithful and true. Since the word Amen means faithful and true, Jesus is repeating himself for emphasis. "I am the faithful and true, the faithful and true." Jesus is Truth, and everything he says is true and trustworthy.

How is Jesus the Beginning of creation? He is the Author or first cause and ruler of creation. By him all things were made (John 1:1–4). This description would have been familiar to the Laodiceans for they had heard Jesus described this way in Paul's letter to the Colossians.

> The Son is the image of the invisible God, the firstborn over all creation... All things have been created through him and for him. He is before all things, and in him all things hold together. (Colossians 1:15–17, NIV)

What is the significance of this introduction? By calling himself the faithful and true witness, Jesus is providing a benchmark against which all will be measured, and the faithless and untrue Laodiceans are going to come up short. By calling himself the first cause or ruler of creation, he's establishing his credentials as our Maker. He who made us knows our true condition better than we know ourselves.

The Laodiceans had an inflated opinion of themselves. They saw themselves as winners in the game of life. However, their Maker gives them a more honest assessment, and his diagnosis is not good.

Revelation 3:15a I know your deeds, that you are neither cold nor hot.

What deeds does Jesus know? *See Revelation 2:19a on page 77.*

What is cold and hot? There's nothing colder than an unfeeling heart deadened by the implacable demands of the law, and there's nothing hotter than a heart burning with the white-hot love of our heavenly Father. To be cold is to live under the stone-cold statutes of the law. To be hot is to live in the sunny warmth of your Father's loving embrace. It's basking in the white-hot passion of God's wild and uncontainable love and reveling in his grace.

What does it mean to be neither cold nor hot? The Laodiceans had not fully submitted to either law or grace.

There's an old story preachers like to tell about an aqueduct that brought lukewarm and unpalatable water to Laodicea. The parallels drawn from this ancient piece of plumbing are fascinating, but the underlying story is a fiction (more on that below).

Jesus is talking about mixture. Cold is cold and hot is hot and the Laodiceans were neither. Had they been living under the death-dealing law, they would have been as cold as corpses, for a rigid law makes frigid followers. And if they had been walking in the sunshine of God's love, they would have been warmed by his grace. They were doing neither.

Revelation 3:15b ...I wish that you were cold or hot.

Why does Jesus wish we were cold? Because the cold law reveals our need for hot grace.

Some have said that being cold means being indifferent to the things of God, but why would Jesus wish that? Others have said that cold refers to cool, refreshing works. But Jesus is speaking about people, not deeds. "I wish *you* were cold."

Cold is what you are when you live 24/7 under a cold and unforgiving law. It's recognizing that God has a zero-tolerance policy, and that he who keeps the whole law but stumbles on one point will be judged as guilty of all (Jas. 2:10).

He sends forth his commandment to the earth... who can stand before his cold? (Psalm 147:15, 17, AMP)

Like an icy blizzard, the unforgiving law is harsh on human flesh. No one can stand before it, and by it all are condemned. So why does Jesus wish the Laodiceans were cold? Because the merciless mirror of God's law reveals our shortcomings and shame. It exposes our nakedness and condemns us as sinners in need of grace.

We know that whatever the law says, it speaks to those who are under the law, so that every mouth may be closed and all the world may become accountable to God... for all have sinned and fall short of the glory of God (Romans 3:19, 23)

You may say, "I'm not perfect, but I'm basically a good person," and the law replies, "You are not good enough. A holy God demands perfection and nothing less. As we hear the chilling rebuke of the law, winter descends. Our hearts are numbed and our mouths are frozen shut. That's the bad news of Romans 3:23, but the good news follows in the next verse: "All are justified freely by his grace through the redemption that came by Christ Jesus" (Rom. 3:24). The law condemns the best of us, but grace redeems even the worst of us.

Why does Jesus wish we were hot? Because he loves us and he wants us to receive his love.

Contrary to what some have preached (myself included), being hot has nothing to do with having zealous faith or being on fire for God or being busy. The problem with approaching God on the basis of zeal is it's all relative. You may think you're hot stuff. "I fast every week and give a tenth of all I have." But compared to the guy who fasts and gives twice as much you're only lukewarm. You may have led 100 people to Jesus, but compared to renowned evangelists like Reinhard Bonnke, you're a lackadaisical slacker.

Even if you were the most on-fire believer in the world, even if you could out-*Bonnke* Bonnke, do you think God would be impressed? Can you imagine the Almighty saying to the angels, "Look at this firecracker! Clear the seat next to Jesus because this guy is *the Guy*." It's not going to happen.

Being hot has nothing to do with whatever heat we can manufacture and everything to do with the burning heart of God. If we are hot, it is because our Father makes us so. His love shines on us, warming us to the very core of our being.

Jesus does not wish the Laodiceans were more enthusiastic or effective, although those are good things. His desire is that they would know and enjoy his love. The message is similar to that given to the Ephesians, but with one important difference. The Ephesians had known but had wandered from the love of Christ. In contrast, the Laodiceans had never experienced it. They had never opened their hearts to the love of the Lord.

Revelation 3:16a So because you are lukewarm, and neither hot nor cold...

How were they lukewarm? They were mixing law with grace and receiving the benefits of neither. This mixing was not a conscious action, for law cannot be mixed with grace. Rather, their mixed-up religion was the fruit of their self-righteousness.

Perhaps you have heard that the lukewarm Laodiceans were apathetic or their works weren't up to scratch. (As though we were qualified by what we do.) Or maybe you've heard that the Laodiceans weren't fully saved. They were half in and half out of the kingdom. (If such a thing were possible.) These interpretations miss the mark. Being lukewarm is not about reaching the right level of zeal or delivering maximum performance. Lukewarm is what you get when you mix hot with cold. It is mixing:

- the new covenant of grace with the old covenant of works
- the new law written on our hearts with the old law written on stone
- the rest of the new with the ceaseless demands of the old
- the unbreakable promises of God with the brittle promises of man
- the liberty of Zion with the bondage of Sinai
- the ministry of no condemnation with the ministry that condemns

A lukewarm person is fundamentally self-righteous. Their attitude is, "I can make it on my own. I don't need God's help." Self-righteousness, in the words of Charles Spurgeon, is a pleasant draught that intoxicates for a moment, but is as "deadly and damnable as the venom of asps and as the wine of Gomorrah."[8] The Laodiceans' problem was not zeal or ineffectiveness but self-trust. They were addicted to the lukewarm drink of homebrew righteousness.

How do we become lukewarm? By preaching cheap law.

The Laodiceans were famously lukewarm, but anyone can be lukewarm. All you need is a little law. In the Bible we find a great law that no one can keep. It's a law to crush egos and silence boasting mouths. But the self-righteous take that great law and cut it down to manageable size. They belittle and cheapen God's law, making themselves lukewarm.

An oft-heard cry is that the modern church is being undone by cheap grace. There is no such thing. (Grace is free or it's not grace.) The real damage is done by cheap law or the lie that "God accepts anything less than the perfect right-eousness of Jesus."[9] Cheap law may be packaged as the pursuit of holiness or the spiritual disciplines. It could be an emphasis on the sacrifices you bring or the promises you make. Cheap law may take many forms, but it invariably bears the unmistakable and nauseating stench of self-righteousness.

Why were the Laodiceans lukewarm? Anyone can be self-righteous and luke-warm, but the Laodiceans were lukewarm because they were Jewish (see Box 7.1). They had left the synagogue, but they hadn't entered the kingdom. They had heard the good news of grace, but they hadn't let go of the law.

Box 7.1: Were the Laodiceans Jewish?

Laodicea was a multicultural city made up of Phrygians, Lydians, Mace-donians, Syrians, Thracians, and a substantial Jewish population of more than 10,000 people.[10] That's a lot of Jews in one place, yet the Laodicean church, unlike the churches in Smyrna and Philadelphia, experienced no religious persecution. There is no mention of a synagogue of Satan and no rebuke for those "who say they are Jews." How was it possible that in a town with so many Jews, the church didn't face a whiff of opposition? The best answer is that the church was full of law-abiding Jews.

The Laodicean church was Jewish in the same way the Jerusalem church was Jewish. But unlike the Jerusalem Jews, the Laodicean Jews were still bound to the law. Lacking a full revelation of what Christ had done, they were stuck between two covenants. This is why Jesus says they were neither cold (fully under law) nor hot (fully under grace). They were living under law and grace, which is like having a cold bath and hot one at the same time.

The Laodiceans were not the only ones. To this day, many remain confused about the covenants. Their confusion manifests in comments like, "We need to balance God's grace with works," and "God gives us grace to keep his com-mands." In the pursuit of balance, mixed-up preachers give mixed-up messages and the result is mixed-up believers. It's like getting an emetic from the doctor.[11]

Revelation 3:16b ...I will spit you out of my mouth.

Who will Jesus spew out? Not members of his own body.

This spitting out passage is sometimes used to terrorize the bride of Christ. "Fail to perform and the Lord will reject you. If you're not on fire, you'll be in the fire!" Such an evil line is a million miles from the gracious heart of the One who is faithful and true.

Some Bibles translate Jesus' words as, "You make me want to vomit." Have you ever vomited up a kidney or a toe? It's a ridiculous notion, yet this is what some fear will happen. "Jesus vomits body parts." Thankfully, this horrendous picture is refuted by scripture:

The one who comes to me I will most certainly not cast out [I will never, no never, reject one of them who comes to me]. (John 6:37, AMP)

Since Jesus will never ever reject those who come to him, who is in danger of being spit out? It's those who are too proud to come. Who will be rejected by Christ's mouth? It is those who deny their need for Jesus. "Those who deny me before men, I will deny before my Father." Jesus is talking about self-righteous hypocrites who scorn grace. He is not talking about Christians.

What makes Jesus sick? The self-righteous mindset that says, "I don't need a thing from you Jesus. You died for nothing."

Perhaps you've heard that sin makes Jesus nauseous. It's not true. Jesus is the friend of sinners. When he walked the earth, he hung out with sinners and ate with them. Sin is no problem for the Lord, for his grace can cure all sin. But grace cannot deal with self-righteousness because the self-righteous won't have it.

In one of the best sermons on self-righteousness, Spurgeon explained the problem:

A self-righteous man does not and cannot trust Christ, and therefore he cannot see the face of God. None but the naked man will ever go to Christ for clothing; none but the hungry man will ever take Christ to be his food; none but thirsty souls will ever come to this well of Bethlehem to drink. The thirsty are welcome; but those who think they are good, are welcome neither to Sinai

141

nor to Calvary. They have no hope of heaven, no peace in this world, nor in that which is to come.[12]

The Laodiceans were full of themselves and exceedingly religious. They were a church of Pharisees and peacocks. They prayed puffy patronizing prayers that would make you sick to hear them, and their bulletin board was a self-aggrandizing montage of all their good deeds (see Matt. 6:2, 5). Their sermons were self-help soliloquies, and their testimonies were all variations on the tune of, "I did it my way."

If you were to ask the Laodiceans why they did what they did, they would pontificate on the importance of charity and duty. "When one has been blessed as I have, one feels a certain obligation to give back to society." Their motives were nauseating.

Revelation 3:17a Because you say, "I am rich, and have become wealthy, and have need of nothing"...

What was the problem? They didn't recognize their need for Jesus.

For the first and only time in the Bible, we hear the Laodiceans speak, and in their few words we hear arrogance, self-assurance, and a vigorous streak of Adamic independence. Theirs is the boast of the self-made man.

"I am rich." If you met a Laodicean at a party, the first thing you would notice was their affluence. Like the Pharisees, the Laodiceans were lovers of money (Luke 16:14). Wealth was their scorecard, the indisputable proof of their accomplishments. "I am rich because I have kept the rules and earned God's favor. My prosperity is a sign of God's pleasure with me." The Laodiceans were winners in the game of life, and they knew it.

"I have become wealthy." There's nothing wrong with being wealthy, for Abraham, David, Joseph and many godly people had wealth. But the Laodiceans boasted that they had *become* wealthy. They were poor, but now they were rich and all credit went to themselves. "Look at how we have turned ourselves around." Their self-commendation reminds us of Ephraim's boast:

I am very rich; I have become wealthy. With all my wealth they will not find in me any iniquity or sin. (Hosea 12:8, NIV)

Box 7.2: What about the aqueduct?

The ruins of a Roman aqueduct

Commentators have long remarked how Laodicea was located midway between the hot springs of Hierapolis and the cold water of Colossae. The Laodiceans, lacking a reliable water source of their own, apparently built an aqueduct to one or the other or both. Depending on who's telling the story, the water that came to Laodicea was either icy cold to begin with and warmed up on *en route*, or it was piping hot and cooled down. In any case, Laodicea's drinking water was lukewarm and undrinkable. It's a good story, but mostly myth.[13]

In the search for spiritual parallels, commentators have tied themselves in all sorts of hydrological knots. The fact is, all the water in the area was heavily mineralized and unpalatable.[14] The supposedly good water that bubbled out of the ground in Hierapolis was so saturated with calcium that it created beautiful white terraces. It may be that Laodicea was a byword for bad water, but Jesus was not writing a travelogue, and his point seems to have been missed: If one desires a drink that is either cold or hot, a lukewarm beverage will not do.

Jesus said, "I wish that you were cold." If you've worked all day under a hot sun, you will know what it is to crave a cold drink. "I wish that you were hot." If you're out in the snow and chilled to the bone, only a hot drink will do. Jesus gets neither from the Laodiceans. Instead he gets a tepid concoction that makes him gag. His expulsory reaction is a vivid picture of how our self-righteousness affects the One who died for us. In view of Christ's matchless sacrifice, our pathetic attempts to justify ourselves are a vomit-inducing gut punch.

In the same way that failure can lead to despair, success can foster pride and self-righteousness, and that seems to have been the case in Laodicea.

"I have need of nothing." The goal of the self-made life is to stand on one's own feet and to live without aid. In this, the Laodiceans had spectacularly succeeded. They were go-getters whose products were known around the world. Nothing could hinder their driving ambition. Not even natural disasters.

Why did the Laodiceans say they needed nothing? In AD60, one of those earthquakes that afflict Anatolia from time to time, flattened several cities including Laodicea. When Rome offered to assist in the rebuild, the Laodiceans refused. They boasted, "We have need of nothing."[15] Unlike the Sardians and Philadelphians, the Laodiceans fixed themselves. Structures built with local funds were stamped with the proud inscription, "out of our own resources."[16] Lesser cities like Sardis might need aid, but not the self-sufficient Laodiceans. And therein lay the problem.

Grace is heavenly aid, but the self-sufficient don't need it. "We have need of nothing." Their pride will not let them receive what God offers. To ask for help would be an admission of failure. "Grace is for losers, not winners like us."

> **Revelation 3:17b …and you do not know that you are wretched and miserable and poor and blind and naked.**

Who are wretched, miserable, poor, blind and naked? The self-righteous.

Who is wretched and pitiful but the one who is drowning mid-ocean and believes they can save themselves? Who is blind but the lost who can't see their need for help? Who is naked but the one who refuses to be clothed with the life preserver called Jesus?

Jesus only called two groups of people blind: the Laodiceans and the Pharisees. What did they have in common? They were both self-righteous. Jesus said the Pharisees were "fools and blind men" (Matt. 23:17). They were blind because they could not discern their true state before God. They were like white-washed tombs, outwardly beautiful but "full of dead men's bones and all uncleanness" (Matt. 23:27). In the same way, the Laodiceans had an outward appearance of success. Their church attracted social climbers, over-achievers, and winners. But

144

the church was a tomb inhabited by the wretched and deceased. There was no life in it because Jesus wasn't there.

Why does Jesus speak harshly to the Laodiceans? Because they are lost and he loves them.

"You do not know," said Jesus. The Laodiceans had no idea they were spiritually destitute. Like the rich man with his barns (Luke 12:18), they were stockpiling their good works, but they were not rich toward God.

Self-righteousness is the hardest sin to dislodge. God help us, but we trust ourselves like we trust the laws of nature, and success only serves to cement our deception. "I did it. I made it. I came, I saw, I conquered." To be disabused of such a powerful lie, we need a stronger truth. Enter the Faithful and True Witness: "You are wretched."

Why did Jesus say they were wretched? Because only the wretched cry out for rescue. And why did Jesus say they were naked? Because none but the naked will ever go to him for clothing.

Some say Jesus spoke harshly because he hates the Laodiceans. In truth, he loves them, as we will see. Others say his harsh words connote anger and condemnation. But Jesus cares for the Laodiceans and wants them to turn around. He didn't write to condemn them but to save them. If his words sound harsh it's because the truth is sometimes hard to hear. It takes a hard truth to dislodge a deep deception, and that's what Jesus dispenses here. In speaking harshly to the Laodiceans, the faithful and true Witness reveals their true condition. He lets them know, in no uncertain terms, that they have fallen short of God's glory.

Of the seven churches Jesus addresses, the Laodicean church is the only one where he has nothing positive to say. This highlights the seriousness of the Laodiceans' problem. They are not told to remember, like the Ephesians, because there is nothing to remember. Nor are they exhorted to hold fast, like the Philadelphians, because they haven't taken hold. Trusting in their own performance, they are truly lost.

Revelation 3:18a I advise you to buy from me...

Why advise? The law drives us, but Jesus draws us. The law whips, but the Lord woos. The law commands, but Christ counsels us like the true friend he is.

The Ruler of all does not demand obedience from the Laodiceans. He does not threaten them with hellfire or damnation. Instead, he draws them aside like a trader in the marketplace with the deal of a lifetime. "I advise you to buy from me." With unexpected generosity, he makes them an offer that's too good to pass up.

Why is Jesus talking like a businessman? Perhaps it is because this was a church of merchants and business people. They understood the art of the deal. "You want to do business?" Jesus said. "Then do business with me."

Is Jesus saying we can buy our salvation? In a manner of speaking, yes.

To buy something is to exchange something we have for something we value more. You might say we buy salvation by exchanging our sins for his forgiveness, but the real exchange is Jesus for us. Christianity is a divine exchange, our life for his. It's the best deal you'll ever make.

But Jesus said they were poor. How can the poor buy anything? Because grace pays for all.

A Jewish listener hearing this invitation to buy from Jesus would have been reminded of an old prophecy:

> Come, all you who are thirsty, come to the waters; and you who have no money, come, buy and eat! Come, buy wine and milk without money and without cost. (Isaiah 55:1, NIV)

The true riches that Christ offers come without cost, or rather, they come with a great cost that he has paid on our behalf. This deal makes no economic sense. We come to him poor and empty-handed, and receive everything in return. We come naked and are clothed. We come hungry and are filled. We come thirsty and are satisfied.

Revelation 3:18 I advise you to buy from me gold refined by fire so that you may become rich, and white garments so that you may clothe yourself, and that the shame of your nakedness will not be revealed; and eye salve to anoint your eyes so that you may see.

Why gold, garments, and salve? Laodicea's fortunes rested on three legs: gold (their banking sector), garments (their world-famous woolen tunics), and eye salve (Phrygian powder).

Jesus counsels the Laodiceans to purchase the heavenly equivalents of their earthly treasures: refined gold, signifying your God-given faith (1 Pet. 1:7); the white clothes of his righteousness; and salve or revelation so that we may see who Christ is and what he has done for us. In short, he is offering himself. This is an incredibly good deal. The gold of Laodicea corrupts, but the gold of heaven endures forever. The moth-eaten garments of Laodicea won't cover your shame, but Christ's raiment will make you righteous. And while rubbing crushed rocks into your eyelids may or may not help your myopia, the revelation of the Spirit will set you free from the blindness of our conceits.

Some might say that Jesus is calling the Laodiceans to lay themselves on the altar of sacrifice, but that's hardly the impression he's giving. He's inviting them to exchange something that won't last, for something of eternal value. He's offering himself and all the heavenly treasures of wisdom and knowledge that are hidden in him (Col. 2:3). It's an unbeatable offer. To paraphrase the missionary Jim Elliot, "The Laodicean is no fool who gives what he cannot keep to gain what he cannot lose."

Does Jesus want us rich? He wants us rich toward God (Luke 12:21).

There are two kinds of people: the self-righteousness who say, "I am rich and don't need a thing," and the spiritually poor who say, "I need Jesus." The first group are rich-but-poor (like the Laodiceans), while the second are poor-but-rich (like the Smyrneans; see Rev. 2:9a).

Jesus encouraged the Laodiceans to buy from him so they could become rich. When you have Jesus, you have the most priceless treasure in the universe. Without him we are poor, naked, and blind. With him we are truly and eternally rich.

Revelation 3:19a Those whom I love, I reprove and discipline...

Who does Jesus love? Everyone, from faithful Philadelphians to lukewarm Laodiceans.

Commentators typically dismiss the Laodiceans as the worst of the seven churches. If so, the good news is that Jesus loves even the worst of us. The Laodiceans were a pompous pack of poseurs. Smug, rich, and full of themselves, they likely had few friends. Yet here is Jesus, the friend of sinners and poseurs, extending the hand of friendship. It is an astonishing display of grace.

Jesus' letter to the Laodiceans is one of the greatest love letters ever written, yet most don't see it. They hear the rebuke and they picture an angry God who's out to punish nonperformers. Read the letter to the end. Hear Jesus speaking to "those whom I love."

I once had a reader tell me that the Laodiceans were disgusting and useless, and perhaps they were. But they were also loved. This part of the letter seems to have been missed. Jesus loved the Laodiceans. That's why he died for them. That's why he wrote to them.

This love is undeserved, no doubt about it. It is so inexplicable, so unreasonable, that some imagine Jesus is no longer speaking to the Laodiceans. "The last few verses of Revelation chapter three are for the other six churches." But that won't wash. The Spirit is speaking to *all* the churches, even the wretched and unlikable ones. Words of correction may be directed to certain individuals, but God's love is for every single one of us without exception.

The Laodiceans thought they merited God's love on account of their all-round awesomeness and good works, but love that is earned is not love. Jesus shatters their illusion by revealing their wretchedness. Then he says, "I love you in your wretchedness." That's love.

The letter to the Laodiceans makes many people frown. "Look at those awful people. God hates them and I hate them too." This letter ought to make us smile and jump for joy. "If Jesus loves these guys, he surely loves me!" This letter is sometimes interpreted as Exhibit A in the Manual on Church Discipline. "Remember what Jesus said to those lukewarm losers." It ought to be recognized as one of the greatest displays of divine grace. "Remember that Jesus loves Laodiceans!"

What does it mean to reprove and discipline? "To reprove is to punish," says the grim-faced preacher. "Jesus punishes those he loves." He does no such thing, and why would he, since he has borne our punishment on the cross? To penalize the Laodiceans, or anyone, would be to diminish his own costly sacrifice.

To reprove means to convict or expose; to discipline means to disciple or train. These activities are connected because one of the ways our loving Father trains us is by turning on the lights and exposing the dangers around us.

The Laodiceans were heading the wrong way. Jesus spoke sharply not to shame them but to save them and turn them around. By revealing the bankruptcy of their self-righteousness and the depths of their wretchedness, he hoped they would come to him for grace.

Pride is a prison. It diminishes us and severs our connection with others and the Lord. The illusion of self-sufficiency fills our mind with falsehoods. "I don't need anyone or anything." Thank God for the true and faithful Witness who speaks truth to our lies. When our conceits have deceived us and our successes have seduced us, thank God for a friend like Jesus.

Revelation 3:19b Therefore be zealous and repent.

If this isn't about zeal, why does Jesus say be zealous? Because Jesus speaks our language.

The traditional view is that the Laodiceans were lazy and half-hearted, but in reality they were as zealous as Pharisees. They weren't apathetic; they were busy little beavers who had pulled themselves up by their bootstraps. They were successful business people, and Jesus acknowledges their endeavor. "You want to be zealous? Then zealously repent. Run from your dead works and come eagerly to my throne of grace." He's not mocking them; he's exhorting them to channel their natural fervor in a healthy direction.

Self-made religion reverses the order of Jesus' words: "Repent and be zealous. Turn from sin then get busy serving the Lord." This is the path to dead works. Heed this back-to-front advice and you'll end up as self-righteous as a Laodicean. The proper order is, "Be zealous and repent." Run, don't walk to Jesus.

How do we repent? *See Revelation 2:5a on page 28.*

Revelation 3:20 Behold, I stand at the door and knock; if anyone hears my voice and opens the door, I will come in to him and will dine with him, and he with me.

Who's knocking on the door? No Roman.

Under Roman law, visiting officials had the power to requisition lodgings for themselves and their entourage. Even though it was an imposition to host, feed, and even pay hungry soldiers, nobody could shut their door. But the Laodiceans weren't nobody. They were a proud people who, in 40BC, closed their doors to a Roman general called Labienus Parthicus. On another occasion, a wealthy Laodicean called Polemo, came home to find the future emperor Antoninus had billeted himself in his house. An angry Polemo kicked him out. His actions captured the independent Laodicean spirit. "Other, weaker Asian cities may roll out the welcome mat to the Roman oppressors, but we Laodiceans are having none of it.[17]

The Laodiceans were famous for their locked and closed doors, and this is one of their more appealing traits. Shutting one's door to a hostile invader is admirable. But Jesus is no Roman oppressor. Although he is the Ruler of All, he does not impose himself upon us. He does not demand that we open our doors and slay the fatted calf for his benefit. Instead, he gently asks us to open our door so that he may come in and dine with us.

Again, grace.

In the Gospels, Jesus promises that if we knock the door will be opened (Matt. 7:7). But the Laodiceans aren't knocking. They're not the sort of people who do. "We have need of nothing." They won't come to Jesus, so the Ruler of Creation comes to them. It is a stunning act of condescension.

The Laodiceans' religion is offensive, yet Jesus is not offended. Their self-righteousness stinks to high heaven, yet Jesus does not withdraw in a holy huff. Nor does he call down fire from above. Instead, he speaks tenderly with loving-kindness.

Those unacquainted with the grace of God make much of the punishment that Jesus will supposedly inflict on underperforming churches. Yet here is Jesus outside the worst church in the Bible hoping to enter and *dine* with them. Was there ever a more breathtaking picture of grace?

By seeking to justify themselves, the Laodiceans had rejected Christ. Yet here is Jesus offering undeserved acceptance. They had spat upon his good name and insulted the Spirit of Grace, and Jesus replies, "Let's eat."

Like that painting? Perhaps you are familiar with William Holman Hunt's classic painting, "The Light of the World." This painting, which was inspired by Revelation 3:20, portrays a crowned Jesus standing outside a door, preparing to knock. There are countless variations on this painting and in none of them do you find Jesus smiling. Typically he looks solemn, even glum, as though he's worried he will not be invited inside. In the original painting, the door has weeds growing around it. It conveys the sense that the door is permanently shut, never to be opened, and that Jesus will turn away sad.

I would like to see a version of this scene that conveys a sense of joyful anticipation. After all, the people on the other side of the door are moments away from the best surprise of their lives. Jesus has come! They are locked in a prison of sin and self-righteousness, but their Deliverer is here.

It's a common experience for religious people to knock on doors and be turned away, but Jesus is not religious. He's not on a mission to win arguments or hand out booklets. He has come to our door via the longest of journeys because he loves us. He is thrilled to be here, and he can't wait to come in.

In the original painting Jesus is holding a lamp. In other versions he is sometimes seen holding a shepherd's crook, as though he's about to hook the leg of a wayward sheep. But that's not the image Jesus gives in his letter. He has come to dine, to break bread, to feast. He should be holding a bottle of wine (the new wine of the spirit) or a bag of food (the bread of life). He could be wearing a party shirt because the kingdom of God is a party (see Matt. 22:2). If the angels in heaven rejoice whenever a sinner repents, you can be sure the Savior celebrates too.

Whose door is it? The door of our hearts.

The letter is for the church, but the invitation is universal and personal. Jesus said, "If *anyone* hears my voice." His invitation is for you and me and everyone besides. Jesus has not come to the marketplace to address the crowd; he has come to your door and mine to meet each of us where we are at. We all must choose what to do with the Savior outside our door.

How do we hear his voice? Jesus' voice is easy to recognize for he speaks words of life and grace. If the message you're hearing releases the life of Christ and the grace of God, then you are hearing Jesus.

The gentle voice of Jesus can be distinguished from the siren song of Self. Jesus says, "Trust me," but Self screams, "Take charge!" Jesus says, "Rest in my love," but Self squawks, "You gotta make things happen." Jesus says, "You have nothing to prove," but Self cries out, "Make a name for yourself." Listen to Self and you'll end up as miserable as a Laodicean; listen to Jesus and you will have peace such as the world does not know.

In this letter we see a radical demonstration of the one-way love that flows from heaven to earth. The Laodiceans are not nice people, but Jesus says he loves them and wants to spend time with them. Jesus does the same for all of us. "If anyone." He loves us just because. Of course, he wants us to respond to his love. There's no point bringing the wine and bread if we're not going to open the door.

How do we open the door? By saying yes to Jesus. That's it. There are no hoops to jump through, there is no fitness test, no entrance exam. Some worry that they have to believe right or muster sufficient faith to enter the kingdom, but your heavenly Father has made it as easy as possible for you to come home.

What if I don't have enough faith? Faith is simply a positive response to Jesus. In the faith conversation, Jesus takes the initiative and we respond. He speaks, we listen. He knocks, we open the door. He enters, we feast.

What does it mean to dine with Jesus? To dine is to enjoy one another's company. It's resting from your labor, leaving the kitchen, and sitting at the feet of Jesus. It's the ultimate happy meal.

The Light of the world and the Life of the party

Revelation 3:21 He who overcomes, I will grant to him to sit down with me on my throne, as I also overcame and sat down with my Father on his throne.

Who overcomes? *See Revelation 2:7b on page 34.*

Who sits on the throne with Jesus? The believer.

> God raised us up with Christ and seated us with him in the heavenly realms in Christ Jesus. (Ephesians 2:6, NIV)

This promise is a present reality for the Christian. God *has* raised us up. God *has* seated us with Christ. The moment you were placed in Christ, you were seated on his throne. And it's a very strange promise to offer to a Laodicean.

The Laodiceans were success stories. They had climbed the ladder and won the jackpot of life only to hear Jesus say, "You're wretched, miserable, poor, blind, and naked." Jesus hit them with a hard word to awaken them to their true state. But having done that, he unexpectedly offers them a free ride. "Stop trying to claw your way to the top and allow me to elevate you to the very throne of God." Who does that? Who offers to promote the proud? This is not a deal we would offer. We'd rather knock the haughty Laodiceans off their high horse and let them stew in the pit of wretchedness for a while. But Jesus is not like us. He bears witness to the truth that humbles the proud, and then straightaway gives grace to the recently humbled. It's as if he's in a hurry, as though he cannot wait to come in and have dinner with the sort of people the rest of us despise.

Truly the world knows no love like his love.

Revelation 3:22 He who has an ear, let him hear what the Spirit says to the churches.

What does it mean to have an ear to hear? *See Revelation 2:7a on page 32.*

What does the Spirit say to the churches? *See Revelation 2:7a on page 32.*

What was Christ's message for the Laodiceans? "I love you guys, but your muddled religion makes me sick. You mix law with grace and make the most unholy concoction. I would prefer you drank one or the other.

"All this boasting about yourselves and your achievements—if you weren't preaching cheap law you'd realize you have nothing to boast about. You say you need nothing. So why did I go to the cross? You are bearing false witness against yourselves. I am the true Witness and I say you're poor, naked, and wretched. Want to be truly rich? Then buy what I'm selling. Make me your everlasting treasure. Want to be clothed? Receive the garments of my righteousness. Want to see? Allow me to open the eyes of your understanding. Want to do business? Then do business with me.

"You act like you don't need anyone, but I long for you. You shut everyone out, but here I stand, knocking on your door, hoping you'll let me in."

What is Christ's message for us? Some say we must balance grace with law as in, "God gives us grace to keep his commands." This toxic teaching will leave you mixed up and lukewarm. It will diminish what Christ has done and leave you scrambling for brownie points.

Jesus would prefer us to be either cold (fully under law) or hot (fully under grace). If you think you need nothing from God, go to the law and allow those righteous commands to plow the self-righteousness out of your heart. Then once the law has revealed your true state—wretched and desperately in need—run to the Lord and receive from the rich supply of his grace.

Perhaps you have bought into a mixed-up message because you are confused about the covenants. You are not self-righteous; you're just unsure about the relationship between the connection between grace and law. There is no connection. It's one or the other. You don't need a little law; you need a lotta grace. You need to hear how much your Father loves you—how he accepts you, is pleased with you, and will never let you go. Indeed, this is the good news we all need to hear. We need to be constantly reminded what Jesus has done lest we drift from our first love (like the Ephesians) or get tempted back to law keeping (like the Galatians).

Success in this world can stroke your ego yet leave you empty and unsatisfied. True promotion comes from the Lord. In his presence there is fullness of joy, and at his right hand there are pleasures forever more (Ps. 16:11).

It is by grace you have been saved. And God raised us up with Christ and seated us with him in the heavenly realms in Christ Jesus, in order that in the coming ages he might show the incomparable riches of his grace, expressed in his kindness to us in Christ Jesus. (Ephesians 2:5b–7, NIV)

The Gospel in the Seven Letters

Imagine two Jesuses—a true one and a fake. How do you tell which is which? You study them carefully and observe that one of the Jesuses looks and talks exactly like the Jesus of the Gospels, while the other is mean, fickle, and violent. It should not be too hard to dismiss the latter as a false Christ, a rotten caricature of the real Jesus. Yet this false Christ is the one who is often portrayed in connection with the seven letters.

Tradition teaches that the Jesus of the letters is displeased and out to punish poor performers. He is a stern taskmaster who commends us if we do well but condemns us if we don't. He pushes us to pray more, study more, evangelize more, and insists we carry out his work with a smile on our dial. No matter how weary or broken you may be, this Christ expects results. Fail to live up to his high demands and you may lose your crown, have your name erased, and be punished with death and damnation.

I wish I was exaggerating, but I encounter this false Christ on a daily basis. I hear about him from confused preachers and burnt-out believers. In the research I did for this book, I saw him behind comments like these: Jesus is looking for intense enthusiasm in attending all church activities (Ephesus), and he rejects those who are less than zealous (Laodicea). He punishes cowardice (Smyrna), complacency (Sardis), law breaking (Pergamum), and compromise (Thyatira). He watches, he threatens, and if we're not totally obedient, he disciplines us in brutal ways.

The message I heard again and again was this: "God has given you a chance to prove you were worth saving, you miserable sinner. So get busy working for the Lord." And how hard must you work? You must be willing to work until you drop for the sake of Jesus, said one preacher. It is only through hard work and bearing up under fiery trials that we are able to save our souls, said another. What was particularly startling was how these pronouncements were passed off as good news. But there is nothing good about the lie that says we must save ourselves or earn God's favor through dead works.

Happily, the Jesus of the Gospels is not like this, and it is *this* Jesus—the one who came full of grace and truth—that we encounter in his letters. How do I know? Because the Jesus of the seven letters walks and talks exactly like the Jesus of the Gospels.

In these letters, Jesus does not introduce a new gospel or teaching. Instead, he repeats many of the things that he spoke about in the Gospels: how he has received authority from his Father, how he is a witness to the truth, and how we need to repent and believe the good news. This Jesus does not condemn sinners; he loves them. He does not rebuke strays; he woos them back. He speaks words of life to the lost. He gives hope to the oppressed and strength to the weary.[1]

Study the seven letters and you will find many quotes, phrases, and images that come straight out of the Gospels (see Appendix 3: Gospel Parallels in the Seven Letters). These prove beyond all doubt that the Jesus of the Gospels is the same Jesus who wrote the seven letters, and that the revelation he gave us on earth did not change after he returned to heaven. The gospel is still the gospel.

But what is the gospel?

The gospel is the good news that God is good and he loves you just as you are with a love that cannot be measured. His love was radically demonstrated on the cross of Calvary, but it is also revealed seven different ways in the letters from Jesus.

In the letter to Ephesus, Jesus is the Good Shepherd calling to his lost and weary sheep with promises of rest and comfort. In the letter to Smyrna, he is the resurrection and the life comforting those facing trials and death. In the letter to Pergamum, he is the Lord-above-all, slicing through lies and ambiguity with the sword of truth. In the letter to Thyatira, he is the exalted Son of God confronting a charlatan to protect those walking in his Father's love. In the letter to Sardis, he is the spiritual Savior exhorting an unspiritual people to wake from their stupor and be clothed in his righteousness. In the letter to Philadelphia, he is the Holy One who opens doors, empowers the weak, and gives names to nobodies. In the letter to Laodicea, he is the faithful Witness who gives a true account regarding the lostness of the lost before inviting himself around for dinner.

What is the common theme in all these letters? It is grace, or God's undeserved favor for all, from the saintliest Philadelphian to the most noxious Laodicean. In none of the letters do you find Jesus making the sort of outrageous claims that are sometimes attributed to him. You just find grace upon grace — grace for salvation, sanctification, and everything besides. Grace from start to finish.

But don't take my word for it. Look at how John prefaces the seven letters with this well-known exhortation:

John to the seven churches that are in Asia: *Grace to you and peace*, from him who is and who was and who is to come. (Revelation 1:4a, italics added)

Before you begin these letters, says John, you need to know that God's heart toward you is full of grace, and his desire is for your peace.

"But John," you may say. "I'm a miserable sinner." And in the very next verse John assures you that Jesus loves you regardless and has freed you from your sins (Rev. 1:5).

"Oh happy day," you say. "I must repay the Lord by serving him faithfully." No, says John. You are not an indentured servant working to pay off a debt to God, for "he has made us to be a kingdom of priests unto God and his Father" (Rev. 1:6).

Do you see? In the space of three verses, John demolishes that old chestnut that says you are a worm who must work to reimburse God for his kindness. You are loved! says John. You are free! You are a priest king!

This is what grace looks like. It elevates the undeserving sinner and makes him a kingly priest in the glorious kingdom of our God.

My purpose in writing this book has been to help you grow in the grace and knowledge of Jesus Christ. What stops us from growing in grace? Unbelief in the goodness of God. Anytime you heed a message that puts the focus on you and your lack, the result is anxiety and fear. But look to Jesus and his abundant supply, and the result is peace and joy.

Jesus is not only the Good News, he is the good news Herald. In his letters, he testifies of himself. He reminds us of *his* faith, *his* works, *his* perseverance because he alone is our Savior. He does not need our help, not even a little bit. So rest from your labors, abide in his love, and do not fear. Whatever your circumstances, the Lord Jesus is mighty to save.

The grace of the Lord Jesus be with all. Amen. (Revelation 22:21)

Appendix 1: When Were the Seven Letters Written?

John received his Revelation while he was in exile on the island of Patmos (Rev. 1:9). To put a date to his writing requires we ask four related questions: Who was John? When did John arrive on Patmos? When did he leave? And who put him there?

Tradition teaches that the John who recorded Revelation was the aged apostle, a.k.a. John the Evangelist, John the Beloved Disciple, or Saint John. But this tradition is not universally accepted. Some speculate that the Apostle John would have been too old (in his nineties) or too dead (having been martyred) to write Revelation. Some say that Revelation was written by a completely different John, an Ephesian known as John the Presbyter.[1]

Yet there are compelling reasons for accepting the traditional view that Revelation was written by the Apostle John. The book bears the mark of apostolic authority (Rev. 1:4); it contains prophecies and quotes that John personally heard from the Lord (Rev. 1:7, 13:9); and it uniquely shares many phrases and symbols with John's Gospel. For instance, in both books Jesus is referred to as the Word of God, the Lamb of God, the true Witness, the Overcomer, and the glorified Son of Man — common phrases that suggest a common author.[2]

Perhaps the strongest evidence of the Apostle's authorship comes from Irenaeus (130–202), the Bishop of Lyons. Among the Church Fathers, Irenaeus stands tall for a very important reason: In a world without Bibles, Irenaeus popularized the Gospels, and the epistles of Paul, John, James, Peter, and Jude. His contribution to the early church was enormous. While heretics like the Gnostics and Marcionites were running amok, Irenaeus pointed the church to writings that he called scripture. Why do we have four Gospels and not three or five? Because Irenaeus said so. "It is not possible that the Gospels can be either more or fewer in number." He was also one of the first to quote from the book of Revelation.[3] Bear in mind this was 200 years before Revelation was officially considered part of the Bible. He didn't call it Revelation but the *Apocalypse*, which is the Greek word for revelation, and the first word of the book.

In the Apocalypse, John saw this new (Jerusalem) descending upon the new earth... John, *the Lord's disciple*, says that the new Jerusalem above shall (then) descend, as a bride adorned for her husband; and that this is the tabernacle of God, in which God will dwell with men.[4]

The author of Revelation, according to Irenaeus, was the Lord's disciple, the Apostle John. John would have indeed been an old man when he wrote it, but Irenaeus records that John lived until the time of Trajan (98–117).[5]

John getting zapped with bolts of inspiration

Having established *who*, our next question is *when*. When was John on the island of Patmos?

Most early church fathers and historians believed that the Apostle John was exiled to Patmos during the reign of Domitian (81–96) and he penned the book near the end of that time, that is, around 95/96AD. However, some argue that John recorded his revelation decades earlier. Before we consider alternative dates, we will briefly review the evidence supporting the traditional Domitianic date.

Once again, we turn to Irenaeus. Irenaeus was born in Smyrna, just down the road from Ephesus, and he was a disciple of John's disciple Polycarp. As John's spiritual grandson, Irenaeus would have heard many first-hand stories about the great apostle from his teacher. For this reason, we can have more confidence in Irenaeus's date than dates proposed by later writers. Irenaeus said that John's apocalyptic vision "was seen no very long time since, but almost in our day, towards the end of Domitian's reign."[6]

Following Irenaeus, Clement of Alexandria (155–215) said that John returned to Ephesus from the isle of Patmos "upon the tyrant's death."[7] Who was the tyrant in question? According to Eusebius, the Father of Church History, it was the cruel emperor Domitian.[8]

Writing in the third century and based on evidence provided by both Christian and secular sources, Eusebius (260–340) confirmed Irenaeus' claim about John receiving his revelation "at the end of the reign of Domitian."[9]

Domitian, having shown great cruelty toward many... became a successor of Nero in his hatred and enmity toward God. He was, in fact, the second that stirred up a persecution against us... (and) in this persecution the apostle and evangelist John, who was still alive, was condemned to dwell on the island of Patmos in consequence of his testimony to the divine word.[10]

After Nerva succeeded Domitian as emperor, the Roman Senate ruled that those who had been banished should return to their homes and have their property restored. "It was at this time," said Eusebius, "that the apostle John returned from his banishment in the island (of Patmos) and took up his abode at Ephesus."[11]

Another third century author, Victorinus of Pettau (250–303), wrote one of the first commentaries on Revelation. Like those before him, he said John received his visions during the reign of Domitian:

When John said these things (in Revelation) he was in the island of Patmos, condemned to the labor of the mines by Caesar Domitian.[12]

In the fourth century, Jerome (347–420), the church historian, said John was banished to the island of Patmos during the reign of Domitian. According to Jerome, John died a very old man some 68 years after the Lord's crucifixion.[13]

Next was Chromatius, the fourth-century Bishop of Aquileia in Italy, who wrote that John "came back, upon the death of Domitian Caesar, from Patmos," the island where he had written the Revelation.[14]

Isidore, the Archbishop of Seville (560–636), was another who said that John "was bundled off by Domitian Caesar to a mine in the island of Patmos, where he wrote the Apocalypse."[15]

By the seventh-century the tale of how and when John got his revelation had been so often repeated that the Venerable Bede (673–735) was inspired to write this beautiful account of it:

It is a well-known story that John was banished to this island by the Emperor Domitian for the Gospel's sake, and it was fitly given him to penetrate the secrets of heaven, at a time when it was denied him to go beyond a certain spot on earth.[16]

For hundreds of years, the consensus was that the Revelation Letters were written towards the end of the reign of Domitian. Yet today there are some who argue that John received his vision decades earlier, even as far back as the night of the Last Supper. Most of these earlier dates can be dismissed as fanciful conjectures.

But one idea that deserves consideration is the possibility that John was exiled and wrote Revelation during the reign of Nero (54 – 68). This conclusion stands on two pieces of evidence. The first is a claim, made by Tertullian (160–220), that the church in Rome was fortunate on account of the apostles who had been martyred there. Rome was the place where Peter and Paul were martyred and "where the Apostle John was first plunged, unhurt, into boiling oil, and thence remitted to his island exile."[17] Since Peter and Paul were murdered by Nero, it is possible that John's boiling in oil and subsequent banishment were also done by Nero. But Tertullian never says this. He simply says, "Rome did it," not "Nero did it," and Rome might have done it at any time.

The other reason for considering the Nero date is that this is what the Syriac Christians believed. In a fourth-century Syriac book entitled *The History of St. John*, we read:

> After these things, when the Gospel was increasing by the hands of the Apostles, Nero, the unclean and impure and wicked king, heard all that had happened at Ephesus. And he sent (and) took all that the procurator had, and imprisoned him; and laid hold of S. John and drove him into exile; and passed sentence on the city that it should be laid waste.[18]

This is apocryphal. Nero didn't destroy Ephesus, and he most likely didn't banish John. But the story passed into legend before reappearing in the preface to Revelation in the Syriac New Testament known as the Peshitta:

> The revelation which was made unto Juhanon the Evangelist, from Aloha, in Pathamon the island, whither he had been cast by Nero Caesar.[19]

Interestingly, the book of Revelation was not included in the original Peshitta but was added in the seventh century by Thomas of Harqel, a Syrian bishop. It was this Thomas who penned the prefatory note above about John being exiled by

Nero. From where did Thomas get his information? He didn't say. He might have got it from the apocryphal *History of St John*, but he certainly didn't get it from the early church fathers. Since Thomas disagreed with the claims of Irenaeus, Clement, Jerome, Eusebius, Victorinus, Chromatius, Isidore, et al., we must conclude that he made a mistake. Writing hundreds of years after the fact in a location hundreds of miles removed from Patmos, Bishop Thomas was out by about 30 years. Nevertheless, many early-daters are prepared to accept Thomas' word ahead of the combined testimony of the church fathers and historians. This would be justifiable if Thomas' date was backed up by corroborating evidence, but there is none.

Not coincidentally, many of those opting for a Nero-date authorship are preterists who interpret the warnings of Revelation as signaling the imminent destruction of Jerusalem and the temple. Thus they have a vested interest in proving the book was written prior to AD70.

Over the past century, preterism has become increasingly popular. As a result, the dating of Revelation has become an eschatological hot potato. Or a shibboleth. If you say John's book was written before AD70, which was the year Titus and four Roman legions destroyed Jerusalem, you may be labeled a preterist. And if you say it was written after AD70, you may be labeled a futurist.[20]

I am partly preterist and futurist, meaning I see some prophecies as fulfilled while others are yet to be. I have written a book promoting both preterist and futurist positions. I trust this makes me something of a neutral commentator regarding the dating of Revelation. I don't have a preterist axe to grind or a futurist dog in the fight. I just want to know when the Apostle John recorded his apocalyptic vision. Having reviewed the evidence for both early and late authorship dates, I am compelled to conclude that Revelation was written in AD95/96, near the end of Domitian's rule. This conclusion is based on the largely consistent views of the early church fathers and historians, but it also reflects my assessment of the external evidence.[21]

Preterists, lacking external evidence to support their early-date claims, rely heavily on internal evidence. That is, they link certain passages in Revelation with other Biblical prophecies that they believe point to the AD70 destruction of Jerusalem. Here are the scriptures typically used to support their early date claim:

1. John's revelation concerns events that "must shortly take place" (Rev. 1:1). When he says, "The time is near" (Rev. 1:3, 22:10), he is referring to the imminent fall of Jerusalem.

The events which John said "must shortly take place" will occur in Asia, not hundreds of miles away in Judea. John was alluding to events that would affect the seven churches, namely the trials and tribulations arising from Roman persecution, Jewish hostility, and pagan idolatry.

2. In the opening chapter of Revelation, John prophesies that Jesus is coming with the clouds and that those who pierced him will see him and mourn (Rev. 1:7). This prophecy is clearly directed to the generation that died in the AD70 fall of Jerusalem. Therefore, Revelation must have been written before AD70.

The "coming with the clouds" prophecy appears several times in scripture. It was first uttered by Daniel (see Dan. 7:13–14), but John would've heard it from the Lord on the Mount of Olives (see Matt. 24:30). This prophecy has nothing to do with Jesus demolishing Jerusalem and everything to do with the Lord ascending to heaven with clouds. It's a fulfilled prophecy, in other words, and John quotes it at the start of Revelation to show that Jesus is in heaven and this is a *heavenly* revelation that he is about to share. This interpretation is consistent with the tone of John's prologue, which is descriptive rather than prescriptive. He's establishing *who Jesus is* not *what Jesus will do*. "Jesus is the faithful witness; Jesus is the firstborn from the dead; Jesus is the ruler of the kings of earth." In short, Jesus is the Risen Lord who sits enthroned in heaven.

3. References to the synagogue of Satan (Rev. 2:9, 3:9) allude to the persecution of the Christians by the Jews in Smyrna and Philadelphia. Such persecution could not have happened after the Jews were slaughtered by the Romans. Therefore Revelation must have been written before AD70.

Except the Jews in Asia were not slaughtered by the Romans. Titus and his legions did not march through the seven cities *en route* to Jerusalem. Titus marched on

Judea from his base in Egypt, and he returned there afterwards. Although a million or more Jews were slain in the rebellious provinces of Judea and Galilee, the Romans had no reason to massacre Jews in other parts of the empire. Indeed, after the Jewish revolt had been suppressed, Titus made a point of confirming the rights of anxious Jews in other cities.

Preterists sometimes say that all Jewish opposition to the church came to an end after the fall of Jerusalem, but this is incorrect. While the Jews had been wiped out in Judea, they remained fully active in Asia and other parts of the empire. Further, history records that the Jews in Asia were active participants in the martyrdom of Christians such as Polycarp.

4. In his letter to Thyatira, Jesus refers to a "great tribulation" (Rev. 2:22). In the Olivet Discourse, Jesus said a great tribulation would precede the fall of Jerusalem (see Matt. 24:21). Therefore Revelation must have been written before AD70.

What does the great tribulation of Revelation 2 have to do with the great tribulation Jesus spoke of Matthew 24? Nothing. There is no connection at all. The former pertains to Jezebel's followers in Thyatira; the latter affects the Jews of Jerusalem. A few chapters later, John refers to those who have "come out of the great tribulation" (Rev. 7:14). What tribulation is this? A futurist would say it is the great tribulation that precedes the Lord's return, while a preterist would say it was the great tribulation that preceded the fall of Jerusalem. (I would agree with the latter.) But note that the tribulation of Revelation 7 has already happened, while the tribulation in Revelation 2 is yet to happen. Therefore, they cannot be the same tribulation. John's Revelation was recorded after the fall of Jerusalem and before the troubles of Jezebel.

5. In his letter to the Philadelphians, Jesus said he was coming soon (Rev. 3:11) and he repeats that promise at the end of Revelation (22:20). This is a reference to Jesus coming in judgment which he did when he sent the Romans to destroy Jerusalem in AD70.

Except Jesus never says he is coming soon, but quickly. This is not a prophecy about timing (for the Son does not know the day or hour) but speed (when his

Father gives the word, he will come without delay). In various parables, Jesus spoke of servants having to wait a long time for their master (Matt. 24:48, 25:5, 19). In these eschatological parables, there is no sense of an imminent return. The master never comes soon, but he does come quickly, speedily, and unexpectedly.

6. In Revelation 11:1, John is told to measure the temple, which makes no sense if the temple in Jerusalem had already been demolished. Therefore Revelation must have been written before AD70.

Wrong temple. The temple that John is told to measure is the *heavenly* temple (Rev. 11:19, 14:17, 15:5). The real temple, in other words, not the manmade copy. In the new covenant, this temple is represented on earth not by a stone building, but the living Church of Christ (Rev. 3:12, see also 1 Cor. 6:19).

7. In Revelation 11:2 mention is made of the Holy City where the Gentiles will tread underfoot for 42 months. In Revelation 11:8 we are told that this is the same city where the Lord was crucified. This is clearly Jerusalem.

Indeed, but how does this prove that Revelation was written prior to AD70? It doesn't. The voice that John hears is repeating a prophecy made by the Lord. Before he was crucified, Jesus said that "Jerusalem would be trampled underfoot by the Gentiles until the times of the Gentiles are fulfilled" (Luke 21:24). That prophecy came to pass when the Romans trampled the city in AD70. The prophecy was true in the time of John, and it remains true to this day.

8. Revelation 17:10 provides a sequence of seven kings, "five of whom have fallen, one is, and one is yet to come." This is a veiled reference to Nero who was emperor at the time John wrote his Revelation.

No other scripture better demonstrates the subjectivity inherent in the analysis of internal evidence than this mystical sequence of seven kings. Who were they? Who was the first king in the list and who was the sixth and sitting king? Early daters claim the kings were Roman emperors and that Nero was the sixth king in the list (even though he was actually the fifth emperor). Later daters, such as the

166

aforementioned Victorinus of Pettau, insist the sixth king was Domitian.[22] Which is it? Take your pick.

Those who support an early authorship of Revelation have a flimsy case that is further weakened by some difficult questions. Why would Nero merely banish John when he beheaded Paul and crucified Peter? If Laodicea was flattened in a quake in AD60, how could it have bounced back to boast, "I have need of nothing" only four or five years later? How could the Ephesians be well-established in the love of God when Paul visited, but be found far from it in just a few short years? How could the Philadelphians "keep his word" and "not deny his Name," prior to the introduction of the Christian-exposing Curse of the Minim c.90/100? Since the church in Smyrna was not planted until after the death of the Apostle Paul in the mid-sixties, how could it have become famous as one of the Seven Churches prior to AD70?[23]

As we have seen, there is no convincing evidence, internal or otherwise, supporting an early date for Revelation. Lacking facts, preterists sometimes turn to logic to press their claim. "John never mentions the destruction of the temple. This seems an incredible oversight. Therefore Revelation must have been written before AD70." Which is like saying John's Gospel was written before the birth of Christ since he never mentions that either.

The absence of evidence is not evidence. Omitting an event is hardly proof that the book was written prior to that event. The Revelation letters were written for the churches in Asia (Rev. 1:11). If John chose not to mention the Roman destruction of Jerusalem, it was because this Jewish story had no relevance to Christians living a generation later in a different part of the world. With persecution and martyrdom on the horizon, not to mention famines and earthquakes, the Christians in Ephesus, Smyrna, Pergamum, Thyatira, Sardis, Philadelphia, and Laodicea had their own problems to deal with.

"The book of Revelation is about the Lord coming or revealing himself in judgment," say some preterists. "And he did this when he destroyed Jerusalem and the temple system. Therefore Revelation must have been written before AD70."

This old covenant interpretation of history was invented by a Jewish priest named Josephus and subsequently adopted by those who have forgotten the dying words of the Lord. "Father, forgive them." God did not send the Romans to slaughter the children of those who killed his Son. Titus and his legions were not agents of God's wrath, and Jesus did not return to earth in judgment in AD70.[24]

One final and desperate ploy must be mentioned. Lacking evidence and unable to make a compelling argument for an early date, some have tried to discredit the Church Fathers, even suggesting that Irenaeus was wrong to say Revelation was written in the late first century. So we can trust Irenaeus to tell us which books to call Gospels, but we can't trust him to nail down the date of John's Revelation. The fact is the early Church Fathers trusted Irenaeus and so should we. His proximity to John makes him a compelling witness for the case of the later date.

Before I began researching this issue, I was under the impression that the date of John's Revelation was contentious and uncertain. I was wrong. Examine the evidence and you will find there is little to debate. Rather there is a substantial and coherent body of circumstantial evidence that some have chosen to ignore.

We can't be 100 percent certain about the dating of Revelation. Too much time has passed to draw an indisputable conclusion. But the facts and the fathers mostly agree: the Apostle John wrote his Revelation "towards the end of Domitian's reign," that is around AD95/96.

Appendix 2: Apostle Paul vs the Nicolaitans

Is it okay for a Christian to attend idol feasts? Next to circumcision, this was the biggest question facing the early church. Gentile-Christians in particular felt enormous pressure to participate in the pagan practices of their guilds and towns. Idol feasts were the places where business got done, and refusing to participate was tantamount to committing commercial suicide. What was a Christian to do?

In the middle of the first century, the Apostle Paul wrote several chapters on the subject in his first letter to the Corinthians. A generation later, the Nicolaitans were encouraging people to go. It's likely the Nicolaitans drew heavily on Paul's grace message. This begs the question: what might Paul have said to the Nicolaitans? The following is one possible answer to this question.

The Nicolaitans: "Go, attend these festivals. It's fine. God knows your heart. He knows you have to provide for your family."

Apostle Paul: "It's not fine at all. What fellowship can light have with darkness (2 Cor. 6:14)?"

The Nicolaitans: "But you yourself said that idols are nothing at all (1 Cor. 8:4)."

Apostle Paul: "It's not the lumps of wood and stone I'm talking about. It's the principalities and powers behind them."

The Nicolaitans: "These feasts are a local tradition, a colorful component of Pergamene culture."

Apostle Paul: "These festivals are a form of devil worship (1 Cor. 10:20). By participating in them you are honoring Satan. How can you encourage such a thing?"

The Nicolaitans: "It's a culturally sensitive way to reach out to your neighbors. Didn't you say something about being all things to all men so that you might save some (1 Cor. 9:22)?"

Apostle Paul: "I never said become an idol worshipper. What sort of witness is that?! What does a child of the Most High have in common with low-life demons? (2 Cor. 6:15–18)?"

The Nicolaitans: "Your letters are hard to understand on this point. We're not even sure if the great Apostle Paul has a clear stance on this issue."

Apostle Paul: "I do. 'Beloved, flee from idolatry' (1 Cor. 10:14). Flee means run the other way. Have nothing to do with the deeds of darkness."

The Nicolaitans: …

Apostle Paul: "How can you be so ignorant on these matters? When the temple priests make their invocations, to whom are they praying? When idol worshippers bring offerings to the temple, who are they honoring? Hint: It's not the Lord. We're supposed to be demolishing demonic strongholds, not funding them."

The Nicolaitans: "It's just a feast…"

Apostle Paul: "There is a war going on and you are fraternizing with the enemy."

The Nicolaitans: "Didn't Jesus say to love our enemies?"

Apostle Paul: "He didn't mean demons! God's plan is for the church to be a beacon in a dark world, but how can we shine if we're hiding in the dark? You are children of the light. Stop acting as though you belong to the darkness" (1 Th. 5:5).

The Nicolaitans: "Okay, worst-case scenario: going to idol feasts turns out to be a bad thing. It's still okay because God's grace will cover your sins. You see? You have nothing to lose."

Apostle Paul: "There is much to lose, and grace is not a license to sin. Grace is the power of God to say no to superstition and bondage."

The Nicolaitans: "It's easy for you to take a stand on this. You're a big-shot apostle. Whenever there's trouble, you leave town. These folks have to live here. If they don't attend these festivals, they'll pay a price."

Apostle Paul: "You think God doesn't know this? You think he won't protect them?"

The Nicolaitans: "Tell that to Antipas (see Rev. 2:13). He took the sort of stand you're making and his neighbors killed him."

Apostle Paul: "To live is Christ; to die is gain. Antipas held fast and now he's in glory with the Lord. I pray that I will have the strength to do the same when my time comes."

The Nicolaitans: "You're weird."

Apostle Paul: "No, I'm a believer. That's the difference between you and me. I trust Jesus will take care of his own; you don't."

The Nicolaitans: "What are you talking about?"

Apostle Paul: "By encouraging people to eat food sacrificed to idols, you are promoting unbelief in the goodness of God. You're saying, 'God can't be trusted.' It's a diabolical message that has nothing in common with my gospel."

The Nicolaitans: "But these Romans carry swords! Make a fuss and they'll chop your head off."

Apostle Paul: "Jesus has a sword too, and I'll put my faith in him over any man in a toga."

The Nicolaitans: "You're so intolerant. Where does your anger come from?"

Apostle Paul: "The Lord. He hates your message (Rev. 2:6). I hate it too."

Appendix 3: Gospel Parallels in the Seven Letters

The words of Jesus in the four Gospels are quoted, echoed, or alluded to many times in the seven letters. These parallels prove that the Jesus of the Gospels is the same Jesus in the seven letters, and that the good news message he proclaimed on earth did not change after he returned to heaven.

Jesus made at least four verbatim statements that appear in both the Gospels and the seven letters:

1. "Do not fear." (Matt. 10:26, 28, Rev. 2:10, and several other scriptures)
2. "He who has ears to hear, let him hear." (Matt. 11:15, Rev. 2:7, and numerous other scriptures)
3. "I will give to each one of you according to your deeds." (Matt. 16:27, Rev. 2:23)
4. "Everyone who confesses me before men, I will also confess him before my Father who is in heaven." (Matt. 10:32, Rev. 3:5)

In both the Gospels and the letters, Jesus spoke about a number of common subjects. He spoke about testing the fruit of those claiming to apostles and prophets (Matt. 7:16, Rev 2:2), the importance of overcoming (John 16:33, Rev. 2:7), being persecuted for the sake of his Name (Matt. 10:17–18, Rev. 2:10), being tested or sifted by the devil (Luke 22:31, Rev. 2:10), receiving authority from his Father in heaven (Matt. 28:18, Rev 2:27), how God is not impressed by the things that impress men (Luke 16:15, Rev. 3:1), having no life apart from him (John 6:53, Rev. 3:1), the works that God requires (John 6:28–29, Rev. 3:2), the lost rousing themselves and coming home to the Father (Luke 15:24, Rev. 3:2), repenting and believing the good news (Mark 1:15, Rev. 3:2–3), returning at an unexpected hour (Matt. 24:50, Rev 3:3), unprepared servants (Mark 13:33–37, Rev. 3:3), confessing our names before his Father (Matt. 10:32, Rev. 3:5), the joy of knowing your name is securely in the Book of Life (Luke 10:20, John 6:37, Rev. 3:5), the blindness of the self-righteous (Matt. 23:17, Rev. 3:17), rich fools (Luke 12:16–21, Rev. 3:17), and being rich toward God (Luke 12:21, Rev. 3:18).

Jesus also used the same metaphors in the Gospels and the seven letters. He spoke about wielding a sword of truth (Matt. 10:34, Rev. 2:12, 16), bearing a light and easy yoke (Matt. 11:30, Rev. 2:24), keys that he alone carried and that gave people access to the kingdom (John 14:6, Rev. 3:7), and building a temple not made with human hands (John 2:19, Rev. 3:12).

Jesus also did some of the same things in the Gospels and the letters. In both we see him rebuking religious Jews who were hindering people from entering the kingdom (Matt. 23:13, Rev. 3:9). We also find him giving people new names (Rev. 2:17, 3:12), and being a witness to the truth (John 18:37, Rev. 3:14).

Finally, in the seven letters we see Jesus revealing himself in ways that come straight out of the Gospels. To the Ephesians, he is the Good Shepherd calling and pursuing his lost sheep (Luke 15:4, John 10:14). To the Smyrneans, he is the resurrection and the life (John 11:25). To the Pergamenes, he is the Lord with a sword (Matt. 10:34). To the Thyatirans, he is the Son of God (Luke 22:70, John 5:18, 11:4). To the Sardians, he is the master who returns unexpectedly (Matt. 24:50, Mark 13:33–37). To the Philadelphians, he is the Holy One who sits on David's throne bearing David's key (Luke 1:32, John 6:69). And to the Laodiceans, he is the faithful and true witness, the Author and Ruler of creation (John 1:1–4, 14:6).

Notes

How to read the Seven Letters

[1] Milton, J. (1996), *Tramp: The Life of Charlie Chaplin*. New York: HarperCollins, pp.92–93.

[2] Ramsay, W. M. (1906/2015), *The Letters to the Seven Churches of Asia and Their Place in the Plan of the Apocalypse, Second Edition*. London: Forgotten Books, pp.31–34.

[3] State-sponsored persecution at the turn of the first century, although somewhat sporadic and perhaps not at the level formerly practiced by Nero, was driven by the lust for money and the ever-present fear of destabilization. To fund his military ambitions, Domitian resorted to "every sort of robbery," said Suetonius the Roman historian, and that included seizing the property of anyone who fell afoul of the law (*The Lives of the Caesars*, 8:12–13). If a Christian in a court of law refused to acknowledge Domitian as lord and god, they could expect to have their assets stolen. And depending on whichever proconsul was trying them, they might also expect to be severely punished.

[4] Trench, R. C. (1886/2015), *Commentary on the Epistles to the Seven Churches in Asia: Revelation II, III*. London: Forgotten Books, pp.229–31.

1. Ephesus

[1] The story is told in Acts 23. The number of angry Ephesians comes from Edwin M. Yamauchi's (1980) book, *New Testament Cities in Western Asia Minor*, Eugene, OR: Wipf and Stock, p.94.

[2] Jerome, *De Viris Illustribus*, 9.

[3] Irenaeus, *Against Heresies*, 3.3.4. See also Eusebius, *Church History*, 3.23.

[4] Hitchcock, R. D. (1869), "Ephesus," *An Interpreting Dictionary of Scripture Proper Names*, New York, N.Y. Website: www.biblestudytools.com/dictionaries/hitchcocks-bible-names/ephesus.html

[5] The original word for holds in Rev. 2:1 is *krateo* which means to use strength. It is derived from the word *kratos*, which means great vigor or power. Source: *Krateō*, 2902, Strong's Exhaustive Concordance, http://biblehub.com/greek/2902.htm

[6] *Eidó*, 1492, Strong's Exhaustive Concordance, http://biblehub.com/greek/1492.htm

[7] *Kopos*, 2873, Thayer's Greek Lexicon, http://biblehub.com/greek/2873.htm. The word is derived from *kóptō*, (G2875) which means a hard and debilitating blow. The Ephesians were literally beating themselves up with work.

[8] The toiling words in Revelation 2:2–3 are more puzzling than they look. In the original language they seem to say, "I know your toil; you have not toiled." This apparent inconsistency has led translators to interpret the toil of verse 3 as *not wearied*, but there is a play on words here. (In fact, there are two: Jesus says the Ephesians *cannot bear* evil men but they *can bear* suffering.) Jesus is saying he knows the Ephesians' wearisome toil yet they have not wearied of their toil. The Pulpit Commentaries explain this interpretation challenge. Source: Exell, J. and H. D. M. Spence-Jones (editors), *The Pulpit Commentaries*, 1897, website: https://biblehub.com/commentaries/pulpit/revelation-/2.htm

[9] The Ephesian church was built on the foundation of Christ's love for them. We know this because of the many times Paul mentions the love of Christ in his epistle to them. "In love he predestined us for adoption" (Eph. 1:5); "Because of his great love for us, God made us alive with Christ" (Eph. 2:4–5); "Husbands, love your wives, just as Christ

loved the church" (Eph. 5:25); "As dearly loved children walk in the way of love, just as Christ loved us" (Eph. 5:1–2); "Let love mixed with faith be yours from God the Father and from the Master, Jesus Christ" (Eph. 6:23). And in case they missed all his instruction, Paul prayed that the Ephesians would be "rooted and established in love and have power to grasp how wide and long and high and deep is the love of Christ" (Eph. 3:17–18).

[10] The Biblical word for repent, *metanoeó*, means to change your mind or think differently. Source: *Metanoeó*, 3340, Strong's Concordance, http://biblehub.com/greek/3340.htm

[11] The word for remove in this verse is *kineō*. It is derived from a word meaning "to go" and is usually translated as move (e.g., Acts 17:28, Rev. 6:14). There are several Greek words in the New Testament that are commonly translated as remove, but this is not one of them. Source: *Kineō*, 2795, Blue Letter Bible, website: www.blueletterbible.org/-lang/lexicon/lexicon.cfm?Strongs=G2795

[12] This does not happen automatically. Jesus preached the gospel to many who heard but did not understand (Matt. 13:13–15). So did the Apostle Paul (Acts 28:26–27). Typically those who were deaf to the Spirit were caught up in the cares of this world or too invested in performance-based religion to grasp what the Spirit was saying. They didn't turn to Jesus because they refused to believe the good news of his grace (see Acts 28:24).

[13] *Nikaō*, 3528, Strong's Exhaustive Concordance, http://biblehub.com/greek/3528.htm

[14] Most of what I write is original but, credit where credit's due, I heard this nugget direct from the insightful Chad Mansbridge of Bayside Church International in South Australia. The bit about standing on Christ's victory comes from Andrew Wommack's entry for "Romans 8:37" in his *Online Bible Commentary*. Website: www.awmi.net/reading/-online-bible-commentary/#/romans/8/37

[15] Hemer, C.J. (1986/2001), *The Letters to the Seven Churches of Asia in Their Local Setting*. Grand Rapids, MI: William B. Eerdmans, p.44.

[16] Quoted in Barclay, W. (1957/2001), *Letters to the Seven Churches*. Louisville, KY: Westminster John Knox, p.7.

[17] In the beginning of the Bible, the Tree of Life was located in a paradisiacal Garden (Gen. 2:9), but at the end of the Bible it's in a city (Rev. 22:2). This has led some to conclude that Paradise is Eden or the New Jerusalem. Others speculate that it's heaven (see 2 Cor. 12:4), or a halfway house between here and there (see Luke 23:43). These speculations are good fun, but unnecessary to the interpretation of this verse.

2. Smyrna

[1] Ramsay, p.17.

[2] Tertullian, *Against Heretics*, 32. See also Jerome, 17.

[3] Hitchcock, "Smyrna."

[4] *Thlípsis*, 2347, Strong's Exhaustive Concordance, http://biblehub.com/greek/2347.htm

[5] Hemer, p.66.

[6] Some might argue that those "who say they are Jews but are not" is an apt description of a Judaizer rather than a Jew. A Judaizer is someone who tries to impose Jewish customs and laws on Christians (e.g., Acts 15:1). When Peter distanced himself from the Gentiles at a meal, Paul rebuked him for trying to Judaize the Gentiles (Gal. 2:14). Although Peter was momentarily misguided, it cannot be said that he had become part of the synagogue of Satan. That diabolical label can only describe those murderous Jews who Jesus said belonged to their father the devil (John 8:44).

[7] Eusebius, 4.15.

[8] In his commentary on Revelation 2, William Barclay lists six slanders that were leveled against the Christians in the first century. (1) On the basis of the words of the Sacrament—this is my body, and this is my blood—the story went about that Christians were cannibals. (2) Because Christians called their common meal the Love Feast, it was said that their gatherings were orgies of lust. (3) Because Christianity sometimes split families when some members became Christians and some did not, Christians were accused of "tampering with family relationships." (4) The heathens accused Christians of atheism because they could not understand a worship that had no images of the gods such as they themselves had. (5) Christians were accused of being politically disloyal because they would not say: "Caesar is Lord." (6) The Christians were accused of being incendiaries because they said the world would end in flames. Source: *William Barclay's Daily Study Bible*, website: www.studylight.org/commentaries/dsb/revelation-2.html

[9] John Foxe (1563/1830) *Fox's Book of Martyrs: Revised and Improved by the Rev'd John Malham, Volume 1*, William Borradaile, New York, p.411.

[10] Ramsay, pp.17–18.

[11] Tertullian, in his *Apologeticus* or *Apology for the Christians*, which he wrote at the end of the second century, said that Christians were happy to swear by the *lives* of the Caesars, but not their *geniuses* or *genii*, which Tertullian said were demons. Source: W. M. Reeve (translator), *The Apology of Tertullian*, London: Griffith, Farran, Okeden & Welsh, 1889, chapter 32.

[12] Suetonius, *The Lives of the Caesars*, 8:13.

[13] Foxe, p.411.

[14] Tertullian, *Apologeticus*, 33.

[15] Yonge, C. D. (translator), *The Orations of Marcus Tullius Cicero*, London: George Bell & Sons, 1903.

[16] Ramsay, p.275.

[17] For more on this lake of fire passage, see my article, "No liars in heaven." Website: https://wp.me/pNzdT-2wA

[18] Eusebius, 4.15.

[19] "You haven't said much about the second death," said one of my reviewers. "Are you being deliberately vague?" Indeed, I am. While I have my own convictions on the subject, they aren't relevant here. What is relevant is what the Smyrneans believed about the second death. Evidently it was a subject that created so much anxiety and fear, that Jesus felt to address it in his letter. What could be more terrifying to a believer than the prospect that they might be ultimately lost?

3. Pergamum

[1] Pliny the Elder, *Naturalis Historia*, 5.33.

[2] At least that's the story as told by Pliny the Elder (*Historia*, 13.21). In his 2016 book, *The Book: A Cover-to-Cover Exploration of the Most Powerful Object of Our Time* (W. W. Norton & Company), Keith Houston notes that animal skins had been used for writing for hundreds of years prior to Eumenes. However, the Pergamenes may have been the first to transform soft leather hide into taut, smooth parchment.

[3] Hitchcock, "Pergamos."

[4] Hemer, pp.80–2.

5 Garnsey, P. (1968), "The Criminal Jurisdiction of Governors," *The Journal of Roman Studies*, 58, (1/2), pp. 51–59. See also Tacitus, *Histories*, 3.68 and Cassius Dio, *Roman History*, 53.13.6–7.

6 In the early second century, denouncing Christians had become such a common occurrence that Pliny the Younger wrote to the Emperor Trajan for advice on how to deal with it. He said that the "contagion" of Christianity had affected many persons of every age and rank and had spread from the cities to the villages and farms. Surely he couldn't execute them all? The emperor replied that anonymous denouncements were to be ignored, but properly denounced Christians were to be tested and punished. Source: Pliny the Younger, *Letters*, 10.96–97 website: http://faculty.georgetown.edu/jod/-texts/pliny.html (accessed June 28, 2018).

7 Ramsay, p.283.

8 Cassius Dio, *Roman History*, 51.20.6–9.

9 "Hieromartyr Antipas the Bishop of Pergamum and Disciple of St John the Theologian," Orthodox Church in America, website: http://bit.ly/2KqqPgc (accessed June 28, 2018).

10 Eusebius (4.15.48) records the names of three others who were martyred in Pergamum: Carpus, Papylus, and a woman named Agathonice. It may be that these three died after Jesus sent his letter.

11 Balak the king of Moab hired Balaam to curse Israel, but after three encounters with the Lord, Balaam prophesied only blessings (see Num. 21–24). King Balak was understandably unhappy with the service rendered and refused to pay. Balaam was in a bind; he wanted the money, but he couldn't contradict God's word without damaging his own prophetic credibility. He came up with a cunning plan that is mentioned nowhere in scripture except here in Christ's letter to Pergamum: he taught Balak how to defeat Israel through seduction and idolatry. Now you know why the Israelites killed the prophet who spoke only blessings over them (Num. 31:8).

12 Irenaeus was the first to connect the heretical Nicolaitans with Nicolas the deacon (*Heresies*, 1.26.3). But whether this means the Nicolaitans were inspired by Nicolas or had perverted his teachings, is a subject of much debate. Clement of Alexandria, a contemporary of Irenaeus', defended the worthy Nicolas and insisted he had no connection with the Nicolaitans (*Stromata*, 2.20). Eusebius the historian also judged Nicolas to be innocent of any link with the heretics (3.29.3). Others have argued that Nicolaitan was a descriptive name unrelated to Nicolas the deacon. It means "victory over the people" or "conqueror of the laity," which sounds vaguely bad. It bears etymological similarity to the name Balaam, which means "he swallows people." Although scholars have offered a number of imaginative suggestions, exactly how the Nicolaitans conquered or swallowed people remains a mystery.

13 The story is recorded in the apocryphal *Acts of Timothy*. A summary of the events leading to Timothy's death can be found on Wikipedia. Source: https://en.wikipedia.-org/wiki/Acts_of_Timothy

14 Baykara, A. (2012), *The Entertainment Structures in Roman Pergamon*, unpublished master's thesis, Middle East Technical University, Ankara, Turkey, p.29.

15 The sadistic innovations introduced into the games by Domitian are described in Terry Deary's 2013 book *Dangerous Days in the Roman Empire* (Weidenfeld & Nelson: London). In their 2011 book, *The Colosseum*, authors Keith Hopkins and Mary Beard estimate that there were 8,000 combat deaths per year in Rome's famed arena. Multiply that figure by the many centuries during which the Colosseum was used as a killing stage, and the total number of deaths in that building can be conservatively estimated as in the

hundreds of thousands. Pergamum was not Rome, but Pergamum was utterly Roman. It is likely that the city's murder rate was substantial. Killing people for fun was not an occasional pastime, but a state-sponsored horror that endured for hundreds of years.

[16] Ireaneus, *Against Heresies*, 1.6.3.

[17] Rules make things simple, but they also take away our freedom to make life-giving choices. The Jerusalem Council did not pass a law; they offered guidelines, which the Apostle Paul expanded on in his first letter to the Corinthians. In his three chapters on the subject (1 Cor. 8–10), Paul made a number of helpful suggestions for dealing with idol food (e.g., don't flaunt your freedom lest you cause others to stumble (1 Cor. 8:9); steer clear of idol feasts (1 Cor. 10:20); don't ask questions about the origin of food bought in the marketplace or given to you by friends (1 Cor. 10:25–27); do everything for the glory of God and for the good of many so that they may be saved (1 Cor. 10:31–33)).

4. Thyatira

[1] Cited by Trench, p.144.

[2] Hitchcock, "Thyatira."

[3] Ellicott, C. J. (editor) (1878), *Bible Commentary for English Readers*. Website: http://bible-hub.com/commentaries/ellicott/revelation/2.htm

[4] Assuming Lydia founded the church, she must've done so 20 to 45 years before the letter from Jesus arrived. If she was still alive, she would've been an old woman—an old woman who heard the gospel of grace straight from the Apostle of Grace.

[5] Trench, p.148.

[6] Barclay, *Letters*, p.47.

[7] Hemer, p.123.

[8] Barclay, *Letters*, p.39.

[9] It may help if we contrast the earthly principle of sowing and reaping with the free favor of heaven. Left to our own devices, we reap what we sow, and this immutable sequence forms the basis of every religion. "Do good and you'll get good. Keep the rules and you'll be blessed." Then along comes Jesus offering us a new way to live. "I want to bless you because I love you." Because of Jesus we reap what we have not sown and we don't reap what we have. This undeserved favor is like nothing on earth and it is very good news. So now we have a choice: we can reap what we have sown, or we can reap what Christ has sown. In rejecting the Lord, Jezebel chose the former. She had a high-minded attitude that said, "I know better. I don't need anything from God." And Jesus replies, "If you won't do it my way, we'll do it yours. You don't want grace? Reap some karma."

[10] A literal translation of Christ's words reads: "I will cast her into a couch" or "I am throwing her into a bed." There's no mention of sickness or suffering, although it's certainly implied. She's going to end up on a sick bed. The image of Jezebel being cast down reminds us of the original Jezebel who fell to her death (2 Kings 9:33), and her son King Ahaziah who also fell and finished his days bedridden (2 Kings 1:2, 16). The implication is clear: What happened to them will happen to her.

[11] I have a webpage listing every New Testament promise guaranteeing the believer's eternal security. At the time of writing there were 132 promises listed. You can find it here: https://escapetoreality.org/resources/eternal-security/3/

[12] What are the bad consequences of straying from the faith? I list them in an article entitled "What happens to Christians who stray?" Source: https://wp.me/pNzdT-1IS

[13] For more on this subject, see chapter 10, "Royal," in my book *The Gospel in Ten Words*.

5. Sardis

[1] Ovid (8AD), *Metamorphoses*, XI.140–144.

[2] Josephus, *Antiquities of the Jews*, 12.3.4.

[3] Josephus, 14.10.17, 24; 16.6.6.

[4] Tacitus, *Annals*, 2.47. Hemer, p.134.

[5] Hitchcock, "Sardis."

[6] Isaiah described the Holy Spirit seven ways; (1) the spirit of the Lord, (2) the spirit of wisdom and (3) understanding, (4) the spirit of counsel and (5) strength, (6) the spirit of knowledge, and (7) the fear of the Lord (Is. 11:2).

[7] The seven spirits are mentioned several times in Revelation. In the opening chapter they are listed in such a way to suggest the Holy Spirit: "Grace to you and peace, from him who is and who was and who is to come (God the Father), and from the seven Spirits (God the Holy Spirit) who are before his throne, and from Jesus Christ (God the Son)…" (Rev. 1:4–5).

[8] *Stērízō*, 4741, Strong's Exhaustive Concordance, http://biblehub.com/greek/4741.htm

[9] Green was no doubt inspired by Billy Sunday's (1862–1935) classic line: "Going to church doesn't make you a Christian any more than going to a garage makes you an automobile." G.K. Chesterton (1874–1936) used to say something similar. "Going to church doesn't make you a Christian any more than standing in a garage makes you a car."

[10] Some interpret Christ's words to the Sardians as a warning to prepare for the Roman destruction of Jerusalem, but that catastrophe had a long lead time and was hardly a thief-like surprise. The Roman legions began wreaking havoc in Galilee a full three years before they began their siege on the Judean capital.

[11] Since Romans wore white togas in their triumphal processionals, some commentators believe the white garments symbolize the believer's victorious life in Christ. This is not a bad interpretation, but the context here is righteousness. Jesus wants us to trade the filthy rags of our self-righteousness for the spotless garment of his righteousness.

[12] In ancient times, cities kept registers of the local population. If you were found guilty of some crime, you risked losing your status and being stripped of your rights. This was the danger facing the Christians. Being falsely accused as law breakers by influential Jews and jealous pagans, meant they could lose their citizenship, their property, and their lives.

[13] "Birkat Ha-Minim," Encyclopedia Judaica: website: www.jewishvirtuallibrary.org/birkat-ha-minim (accessed June 28, 2018).

6. Philadelphia

[1] Ramsay, pp.391–2.

[2] Strabo, *Geographica*, 13.4.10.

[3] Demetrius is identified as the first bishop of Philadelphia in Clement's *Apostolical Constitutions*, 8.46.

[4] Easton, M.G., (1893), "Philadelphia," *Easton's Bible Dictionary*, website: www.biblestudytools.com/dictionary/philadelphia/

[5] God is acknowledged as the Holy One of Israel in the Psalms (71:22, 78:41, 89:18) and more than two dozen times in Isaiah and a few other places. He is called the God of Truth in Psalm 31:5 and Isaiah 65:16 and the true God in 2 Chronicles 15:3 and Jeremiah 10:10.

[6] Who were these eleven Philadelphian martyrs (Eusebius, 4.15.45)? Nobody knows. Unlike Polycarp, their names have been forgotten. Chances are they were ordinary believers.

[7] Ignatius, *Epistle to the Philadelphians*, 6.

[8] Quickly (*tachu*) means quickly or speedily. By implication it can mean soon, but that cannot be the case when describing the Lord's return (see Matt. 24:48, 25:5, 19). Source: *Tachu*, 5035, Thayer and Smith Greek Lexicon, www.biblestudytools.com/lexicons/-greek/kjv/tachu.html

[9] Trench, p.190.

[10] Jesus told the Philadelphians that he would name them "the city of my God." Interestingly, the modern name of Philadelphia is Alaşehir, which means city of God.

[11] For a fuller understanding of the difference between the covenants, see my ebook *What Makes the New Covenant New?* You can get it free here: https://escapetoreality.org/-subscribe/

7. Laodicea

[1] Ramsay, p.414.

[2] Save an airfare and check it out on Google Earth.

[3] Strabo, 12.8.16.

[4] Ramsay, p.429.

[5] The letter is addressed to "the angel of *the church* in Laodicea" (Rev. 3:14). The original word is *ekklesia*, which is usually translated as church but not always. Sometimes it can refer to a group of people meeting together (see Acts 19:32, 39, 41), and perhaps that was the case in Laodicea.

[6] Hitchcock, "Laodicea."

[7] Archippus of Colossae is identified as the first bishop of Laodicea in Clement's (375–380AD) *Apostolical Constitutions*, 8.46.

[8] Spurgeon, C.H. (1860), "A Blow at Self-Righteousness", Metropolitan Tabernacle Pulpit Volume 7, Sermon No. 350. Website: www.spurgeon.org/resource-library/sermons/a-blow-at-self-righteousness (accessed June 28, 2018).

[9] Tullian Tchividjian popularized the concept of cheap law in a 2012 Christian Post article (website: www.christianpost.com/news/cheap-law-76378/). In his 2013 book, *One Way Love: Inexhaustible Grace for an Exhausted World* (David C. Cook), Tchividjian wrote, "Contrary to what some Christians would have you believe, the biggest problem facing the church today is not 'cheap grace' but 'cheap law' — the idea that God accepts anything less than the perfect righteousness of Jesus…A high view of the law produces a high view of grace. A low view of the law produces a low view of grace" (pp.97–98).

The concept of cheap law was introduced by Gerhard Forde (1927–2005) as a response to Dietrich Bonhoeffer's (1906–1945) well-known rebuke of cheap grace. Cheap grace, according to Bonhoeffer in his 1963 book *The Cost of Discipleship*, (New York: Collier), leaves sinners unchanged and gives rise to moral laxity. The remedy is to preach costly grace, meaning grace with conditions. Forde vigorously resisted this idea. "Wherever grace is made to become more costly the law must be cheapened," (quoted in Lazar, S.C. (2013), "Cheap grace or cheap law? Dietrich Bonhoeffer and Gerhard Forde on the nature of law and gospel," *Journal of the Grace Evangelical Society*, 26(50), p.25). The fundamental problem with cheap law is "it nullifies grace," said John Dink in a 2012 essay. "Cheap law weakens God's demand for perfection, and in doing so, breathes life into the old creature and his quest for a righteousness of his own making" (Source: "Hallelujah! What a Savior," website: https://johndink.wordpress.com/-2012/05/25/hallelujah-what-a-savior/).

[10] Jews had been living in the Lycus Valley for hundreds of years. In the second century BC, Antiochus III had 2,000 Jewish families relocated there from Babylon. Two hundred years later, but still well before the birth of Christ, the proconsul Flaccus confiscated from them a large amount of gold that had been collected to pay the temple tax. The gold was worth 15,000 days' wages. Since the temple tax was the equivalent of two days' wages, there must have been at least 7,500 Jewish men in the district (not counting women and children) (Ramsay, p.420). Fast forward 100 years to the time of the seven letters and the Jewish population would have been higher still. "So many Jews came to live in the part of Asia," wrote Barclay, that even "the Jews of Jerusalem were moved to complain about the number of Jews who had forsaken Palestine for the luxuries and baths of Phrygia" (*Letters*, p.80).

[11] The mixture of unmixable things is a leading cause of complacency in the church. If Christians are lukewarm in the modern sense of the word, it's because they are lukewarm in the Biblical sense of the word. They've been paralyzed by the irreconcilable demands of mixture.

[12] Spurgeon, *Self-Righteousness*.

[13] Laodicea was located at the junction of two small rivers that merged into the Lycus River. According to Strabo, these rivers supplied drinkable water (13.4.14). It's true the growing town came to rely on an aqueduct—as did Ephesus, Smyrna, Pergamum, and Sardis—but the aqueduct didn't link Laodicea with either Hierapolis or Colossae. Nor is there any evidence that the water taken from the aqueduct was objectionable on account of its temperature. Source: Koester, C.R. (2003), "The Message to Laodicea and the Problem of Its Local Context," *Faculty Publications*, 9, Luther Seminary. Website: http://digitalcommons.luthersem.edu/faculty_articles/9 (accessed June 28, 2018).

[14] After studying the archeological and historical literature, Hemer concluded that upper Lycus River Valley was noted for "both the abundance of water in the district and its bad quality" (p.189).

[15] Tacitus the Roman senator recorded: "One of the famous cities of Asia, Laodicea, was that same year (60AD) overthrown by an earthquake, and, without any relief from us, recovered itself by its own resources" (*Annals* 14:27).

[16] Hemer, p.195.

[17] These two stories of Roman imposition are recounted by Hemer (pp.204–5).

The Gospel in the Seven Letters

[1] In my reading, I found many commentators were quick to identify parallels between the seven letters and the Old Testament, but very few made any connection with the Gospels. Perhaps this explains why so many were pushing a mixed message of grace plus works. Read a new covenant book through an old covenant lens, and you'll end up confused.

Appendix 1: When were the Seven Letters Written?

[1] This conjecture originated with Papias, the Bishop of Hierapolis (60–163AD) and a contemporary of Polycarp's. Nothing Papias wrote has survived in its original form, but fragments of his work are quoted by Eusebius in his seminal *Church History* (3:39). In one such fragment Papias names several church leaders including two Johns. Was he referring to two different people, or was he naming the same John twice? Eusebius concluded that Papias had listed two Johns and concedes that the latter one—John the Presbyter—may have written the book of Revelation. However, Eusebius also records that the Apostle John was alive and well at the end of the first century and governing the churches of Asia (3:23). It was this John—John the Lord's disciple—who mentored Papias, or so said Irenaeus, writing more than a hundred years before Eusebius (*Heresies*, 5.33.4). And what of the second John? The one called Presbyter? Irenaeus never mentions him.

[2] In both John's Gospel and his Revelation, Jesus is described as the Word of God (John 1:1, Rev. 19:13), the Lamb of God (John 1:29, 36, Rev. 5:6 and numerous other references), the true Witness (John 1:7, 8:14–18, Rev. 3:14), the Overcomer (John 16:33, Rev. 17:14), and the glorified Son of Man (John 12:23, 13:31, Rev. 1:13–15).

[3] Irenaeus, *Heresies*, 3.11 and 4.20.

[4] Ibid, 5:35.

[5] Ibid, 2.22.5.

[6] Ibid, 5.30.3.

[7] Clement, *Who is the Rich Man That Shall Be Saved?* 42.

[8] Eusebius, 3.23.

[9] Ibid, 3.18.2–3.

[10] Ibid, 3.18.1.

[11] Ibid, 3.22.10–11.

[12] Victorinus, *Commentary on the Apocalypse*, 10.11.

[13] Jerome, 9.

[14] Chromatius, *Sermons on the Gospel of Matthew*, 1.

[15] Quoted in the *Commentary on the Apocalypse* by Beatus of Liebana, translated by M.S. O'Brien (2015).

[16] Bede, *The Explanation of the Apocalypse*, 1.9.

[17] Tertullian, *Heretics*, 36.

[18] Wright, W. (1871), *Apocryphal Acts of the Apostles*, website: https://archive.org/details/-apocryphalactsa00wriggoog (accessed June 28, 2018).

[19] Etheridge, J.W. (1846), *The Peschito Syriac New Testament*, website: http://aramaicnew-testament.org/peshitta/etheridge/epistle/revelation_1.htm (accessed June 28, 2018).

[20] A preterist is someone who believes biblical prophecy has been fulfilled. Some preterists, not all, believe the warnings of Revelation point to the AD70 destruction of Jerusalem and the temple. In contrast, a futurist is someone who believes prophecy is yet to be fulfilled. Some futurists, not all, believe the warnings of Revelation point to a future tribulation.

[21] To reconcile the strong evidence in support of a Domitianic date for the writing of Revelation with the preterist desire for a pre-AD70 date, some have speculated that the teenaged Domitian ruled Rome as a de facto emperor in his father's name in the early months of AD70. It's an interesting idea but it lacks any basis in fact. Vespasian was declared emperor by the Roman senate in December 21, 69. He was in Egypt at the time,

so Vespasian delegated the empire's administrative responsibilities to the capable and loyal general Mucianus. Mucianus ran Rome for the few months it took for Vespasian to travel to the capital. At no time was Domitian in charge. Even if the teenager had got his hands on the tiller of state, he would not have had time to do half the things preterists claim. Fourteen weeks—that's how much time transpired between the promotion of Vespasian and the commencement of the Jerusalem siege. The preterist interpretation thus requires us to believe that in the space of three months John was arrested, exiled, and received and wrote his vision before circulating it among the seven churches so that they could be warned to flee from Romans, who were apparently sprinting ultramarathons across Asia killing every Jew they met.

[22] In his *Commentary on the Apocalypse* (17:10), Victorinus says the sequence of seven kings "must be understood in (the time period in) which the written Apocalypse was published." Since Domitian was on the throne, the five who had fallen before him were Titus his brother, Vespasian his father, and Otho, Vitellius, and Galba. The one who is yet to come and who remains only a little while is Nerva, who lasted less than two years.

[23] In his *Letter to the Philippians*, Polycarp said the Smryneans had not known the Lord during the time of Paul (11:3).

[24] For 2,000 years, theologians such as John Chrysostom, John Calvin, Matthew Henry, John Gill, Adam Clarke, George Holford, and others have followed Josephus in blaming God for the Roman destruction of Jerusalem and the temple. However, the traditional view that God abandoned the nation of Israel in punishment for killing his Son is refuted by scripture. "Did God reject his people? By no means!" (Rom. 11:1). God did not punish Jerusalem; he redeemed it. He made that Christ-killing city Ground Zero for the gospel and his church. For more, see my article, "Jesus for Jerusalem." Website: https://-wp.me/pNzdT-3tf

Scripture Index

Image Credits

Unless otherwise stated, all images are public domain, Creative Commons license, or considered fair use. The original portraits of John (p.15), Polycarp (p.40), and Irenaeus (p.64) were done by Pakhin Thanathornthana. The Seven Churches (p.20) is a detail from the Seven Churches in Asia, a stained glass in York Minster by John Thornton. The bust of Domitian (p.47) is from WikiCommons. The Crown of Smyrna (p.49) is from Mark Twain's 1969 book *Innocents Abroad*. The citadel of Sardis (p.106) is by Charlene Caprio (used with permission). The Aqua Claudia aqueduct (p.143) is from the 1911 Encyclopedia Britannica. The modified version of William Holman Hunt's "Light of the World" (p.152), is by Blenk. John getting zapped (p.160) is better known as "St John the Evangelist on Patmos," by Titian (1490–1576).

Acknowledgements

Letters from Jesus was slow-cooked over a period of ten years. Bits of this book were tested on my blog, and I am grateful to the many Escape to Reality readers who provided feedback and encouragement.

The entire book was read by three friends. Chad Mansbridge, Dave Orrison, and Ed Elliott provided valuable input for which I am enormously grateful. Of course, any wonky theology that made it into the book is my fault, not theirs.

The talented Rémi Torralba made the map of the Seven Churches; Jelena Mirkovic Jankovic designed the front cover and Brad Wallace did the back; Shelly Davis and Roxana Coumans did the proofreading; and my beautiful wife Camilla helped in more ways than I can count.

I write full-time about the gospel of grace, and most of what I write is given away for free. Thanks to the generosity of patrons on Patreon, the good news that I preach is heard in every country on earth. Patrons are partners in this gospel, and without their support, books like this would not be possible. For sharing the journey, heartfelt thanks to Swee Heng Chee, Randy and Julee Armstrong, Charles and Sheilla van Wijk, Terry Maupin, Bill Fowler, Michael and Julie Lipparelli, Ben Dailey, Henry Yeo, Richard Bradford, Doug Hignell, Albert Pak Kwan Soo, Rachmat Permana, Thomas Ludemann, Kris Page, Don Beeson, Amanda Henderson, Ian and Norma Anderson, Jean-Paul Parenteau, Terence Koh, John Williams, Tony Vogel, Jason Whitaker, Justin Hopper, Agnes Tan,

Klaus and Erika Degen, Erik Grangård, Jason Kim, Michael and Kimberly Vizza, Ted Nelson, Sandra Osei-Gyamfi, Peter Hanson, David Edwardds, Marion Carter, Farrah Cox, Mikael Jonsson, Jerry Williams, Derrick Darden, James Tuttle, Miguel, Stephanie, and Estelle Gonzalez, Marisa Raynaldo, Terry Myers, Steve Chui Hom Lap, James A Mullier, Cecilia Villanobles Lim, Gerry Macabuhay, Julia Vockrodt, Randy Parry, Keith Pinke, Anne H Hoover, Keith Forwith, Anne T Ross, Marshall Kim, Jack Surrett, Low Jer Wei, Deirdre M Rogers, Dottie Hicks, Tom and Kay Stocking, Viwe Jafta, Christopher Gordon, Norin Lumungking-Weier, Steven J Shane, Robin M Waller, Cesar and Anna Ceneviz, Randall Harmon, Steve and Sandra McCollom, Daniel Goodlin, the Georgeff Family, Kenneth Crum, Elly "Singer" Kraai, Jan Kiel, Christopher Johnson, Rebekah K Watson, James A Young Jr., James Davis, Real Paquette, Ricky L Cain, Bruce Leane, Susie Dunlap, Lloyd D McCaskill, Nick Atkins, Steven Kotsonis, Jeffrey, Rene Bouwer, Lester Blair, Nancy Reed, Gord Penner, Paul Noble, Andy Manuel, Benny Sunjaya, Damon Jackson, Janice Best Bright, Brandon Petrowski, Toshiko Johnson, Lyle Geck, Michelle Nonis, Alan Pearson, Shannon Carroll, John Adriaans, Josh Klaas, Reverend Oscar Rios, Patty VanderVeen, J Bradley Reed, Rocky Waenga, Adriaan Hattingh, Werner and Bonnie Olivier, Dennis and Denise Capra, Kim Geisnes, Samuel Lowell, Jana Mings, Georg Zönnchen, Tony Portell, Geraldine Unger, Peta Donegan, Pagasa De Mesa, Jose Moya, Corinna von der Mühlen, Suzanne Sherritt, James W Smith, Eveline Hotz Gamonez, Bruce Chittick, Moses S M Kawuma, Helen Teichroeb, Jim Gaines, Susan Pawlowski, Raymond Glossop, Diane Peterson, Ann Burns, Pat Greene, Mary Ellen Serafine, Craig Hunt, Deborah Long, Elias Struik, Adam Tanti, Edward McCarthy, Denis Paquette, Mark Flint, Liz Bailey, Melissa Keewee, Marie, Rhea Cooper, Richard Lee, Mark McElwee, Bank Akinmola, Chad Huffman, Cory Smith, Diane Schakola, Larry and Helen Wilgus, Mary Salisbury, Carl and Sara Petee, Tanya Nareau, Leanne Hopkins, Gilly Stott, Renee Woodward, Adebare Adedigba, Jenna B North, Bev Setterberg, James Goss, Brian Page, Jax Hill, S Kunnath, Mary Anne Tango, Kimberly Russell, Asit Parida, Ed Elliott, Carol Milhous, Leon C Bramlett III, Lidia, Marios Pontos, Bob Paroski, Michael Gragg, Jordan Hammond, Stephen Caldwell, Bruce Fulton, Shelly Hakspiel, Cecil H Paxton, Clint Byars, Dave Feather, Jonathan Gould, Leonard John Ransil, Graham Arthur Purkis, Melanie Theilig, Kent Gilge, Johanna Cappon, Mark Steenhoff, Michael Scroggs, Adam Goldfinch, Alison Gilbert, Maggie Fitzpatrick, Matthew Sr, Lew Gervais, Luc Constantin, Heather Gill, Harry Finn, Bruno Dammann, Jan Jarmon Bingaman, Dollice Chua, Sara Wilson Hughes, James Miller, Paul Woodrich,

ACKNOWLEDGEMENTS

Tony Ide, Chad M Mansbridge, Eric and Nancy Holman, Will McCulloch, Brian Spears, Dave Tremblay, Christopher Molle, Daniel Cox, Kristi Gorrod, Connie-Louise Alexander, Leon Minton, Dawn Strom, Simon Brown, Jonathan and Christina Ybarra, Eric Thon, Max Soutter, Jason Foo, David Wong, Andre de Haan, Hannah Hoffmann, Randall George, Ronja White, Michael Kelehan, Jay Treat, Kathy Haecker, Helen Kearney, Andrew Ys, Alonzo Garcia, Michelle, Ronan, Kenneth Hamner, Tommy Bason, Richard F De Souza, Robert Marshall, Gilbert Gatdula, Cherine Rossman, Ron Clark, Bik Hou, John Gardner, Ed Rasmussen, Gary Wells, Aney Mathew, Lauri Kinnunen, Norah Brown, David Aaleskjaer, Timothy Warden, Ed Crenshaw, Peter Sinish, Roger Staubus, Millie Morrison, Janet Andersen, Penny Creery, Kev Ngawhau, Rachel Peters, Scott Boyd, Nata Isr, Greg and Raelene Race, Richard Elson, Emanuel Bulugu, Eddie C Livingston P.E., Lois Granbery, Michael Morimando, Todd Hardy, Dale Edwards, David Nelson, Chris Esparza, Red Burgos, Jennifer and Mike Matwijec, Lee Tyler, Annalee Reyes, Toluwalope Ariyo, Debra Hardy, Richard W Evans, Julie Decker, Darrell Alexander, Thierry Bras, Roshan Easo, Evelyn Reyna, Dennis Plum, Michael Folsom, Jan Hoke, Bob Fricke, Uschi de Bruyn, James Geluko, Michael Styron, Thomas E Wiseman, Garry D Pifer, Esther van Dijk, Jhazz C, Lisa Reveley, Brian Jones, Michelle Lavette French, Robert Jones, Wesley Matsell, Marcos Roi Gomez, Nancy Paquette Poulin, Matthew Weyers, Matthew Thiele, Lee Ping Tung, Tim Brasic, Leroy Herring, Jeremy Pelfrey, Bill McDonald, Alyssa Wenzel, Brian Campbell, Stephanie Turney, David Dunham, Kundayi Bernard Mugabe, Carolyn Fewster, Peter Barnett, Kit Mafu, Emanuel Norlin, Anita Sheridan, Chucks Obinna Ugoihe, Joel Belcher, Gary Greer, Janelle Myers, Ben Shipton, Caleb Mitre, Andrew Babu, Brian McLaughlin, Hazel Saquing, Lisa Rios, Patti McPike, Yuting Kita, Nagy Andrea Eva, Stacey Todd, Paul De Sousa, Carol Sitzlar, Anders Ohlsson, John Ross, Mario Magallanes, Berris-Dale Joseph, Natalie, Falxion, Phelim Doherty, Kirsty Gerlach, Josh King, Olen Jones, Katelyn Hellenbrand, Makala Doulos, Larry Elegado Gracilla, John Sam, Marius Alin Sbingu, Dennis Odavar, Stefanie Esparza, Steve Douglas, Buddy Palmer, Hannu Tapani Honkapää, Megan Urlaub, Madeline McHugh, Colin Leo, Rudi Scheele, and David Chin.

www.patreon.com/escapetoreality

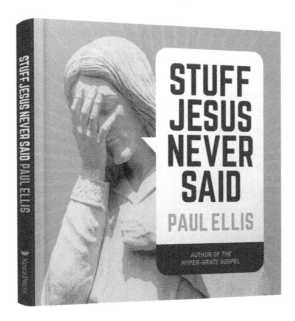

Other books by Paul Ellis

The good news may be the best news you never heard!

Discover the secret to walking in divine favor and experiencing freedom in every aspect of your life. Learn who you really are and why you were born. *The Gospel in Ten Words* will transport you to the heavenly treasure rooms of grace leaving you awe-struck at the stunning goodness of God.

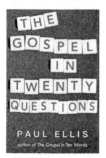

A good question can change your life!

Questions are keys to treasure and doorways to discovery. *The Gospel in Twenty Questions* will cause you to dance on the uplands of your Father's favor. The questions in this book will lead you to a deeper relationship with Jesus, the greatest Answer of all.

God's love for you is greater than you know!

Drawing on insights gleaned from more than forty grace preachers, *The Hyper-Grace Gospel* addresses common mis-perceptions some have about the message of grace. This book will leave you marveling at the relentless love of your Father.

AVAILABLE NOW!

Amazon, BAM!, Barnes & Noble, Book Depository, Booktopia, Eden.co.uk,
Kinokuniya, Loot.co.za, Nile.com.au, Waterstones, W.H. Smith,
and other good retailers.

www.KingsPress.org

Made in the USA
Monee, IL
03 May 2022